Creative
FINISHING TOUCHES
WITH PAINT

Cover pictures: (l) Marie Claire Idées/G. de Chabaneix/
C. de Chabaneix/M.C. Bastit; (tr) Eaglemoss/Graham Rae;
(br) Marie Claire Idées/C. Fleurent/P.Chastres.

Page 1: Ariadne Holland; page 3 IPC Magazines/Robert Harding
Syndication/Tom Leighton; page 4 IPC Magazines/Robert Harding
Syndication/Joshua Pulman; page 5 Eaglemoss/Jonathan Pollock.

Based on *Creating Your Home*
published in the UK by
© Eaglemoss Publications Ltd 1996
All rights reserved

First published in North America
in 1997 by Betterway Books,
an imprint of F&W Publications, Inc.
1507 Dana Avenue
Cincinnati, Ohio 45207
1-800/289-0963

ISBN 1-55870-450-7

Manufactured in Hong Kong

10 9 8 7 6 5 4 3 2 1

Creative FINISHING TOUCHES WITH PAINT

BETTERWAY BOOKS

Contents

CREATE RICH FAUX FINISH EFFECTS

Paint brushes and tools   *7*

Crackleglazing   *9*

Paint distressing   *13*

Embossed effect frames   *17*

Gilding   *19*

Quick gilding   *23*

Liming wood   *27*

Marble paint effects   *31*

Faux marquetry   *35*

Stippling   *39*

Verdigris paint effects   *43*

Woodgraining   *47*

DISCOVER THE EASE OF STENCILING AND PRINTING

Stenciling on wood   *51*

Creating a stencil   *55*

Spray paint stenciling   *59*

Textured stenciling   *63*

Decorating floorboards   *67*

Mosaic block printing   *73*

TRY HAND PAINTING FOR A PERSONAL TOUCH

Furniture facelifts   77

Hand painting designs   81

Painted fireplaces   87

Decorative lining   89

Pots of color   93

ADD COLOR WITH PAINTED ACCESSORIES

Painting china and glass   95

Traditional decoupage   97

Glass decoupage   101

Curved glass decoupage   103

Decoupage firescreen   107

Mouldings for character   111

Papier mâché containers   115

Papier mâché accessories   119

Coloring wickerwork   123

INDEX   127

Using the right brush or tool is important for all types of paintwork, in particular decorative paint effects.

The brushes or tools you choose and how you use them are the deciding factors for all types of paint effects. The shape and size of the brush or tool, what it's made of, and the way you use it to apply and manipulate the paint determine the look and subtlety of the finish. If possible, use the recommended item and always experiment on an inconspicuous area of the surface being decorated.

artists' brushes

Brushes

Specialist brushes can be expensive, but they are an investment if you are planning a fair size project or to use them more than once. Good quality brushes give better results and last longer. For small jobs, you can substitute cheaper types of brushes.

Artists' brushes These are small brushes for fine decorative work and for painting details such as faux marble veining and woodgraining. The bristles can be soft (made from sable, camel hair, squirrel or synthetic fibre) or coarse (made from hogshair or synthetic fibre). They are available in a wide variety of shapes, which largely determine the marks they make.

Decorators' brushes Standard decorating brushes are invaluable for large scale painting, applying glazes, painting walls and pasting paper. Sizes range from 12-150mm (½-6in).

Dragging brushes/floggers These coarse, long-bristled brushes create a streaky, woodgrain effect in wet glaze. The good ones are made from horsehair and are available in sizes 7.5-15cm (3-6in) wide. A less expensive alternative is a coarse decorators' brush.

Dusting brushes These are soft brushes with medium length, densely packed bristles used for small stippling projects and for softening glazes and colour washes. They are less costly than badger hair softening brushes but don't give the same soft bloom of colour.

Fantail brushes These are one type of soft artists' brush with fine, splayed bristles. They are used for softening brush marks in woodgraining, marbling and grisaille. As an alternative, use a soft artists' brush.

Fitches These are artists' brushes with stiff bristles and round, pointed or flat heads. They are ideal for adding detail in oilwork, small-scale stippling and stencilling. Sizes vary from 3-30mm (⅛-1¼in) wide. *Lining fitches* have diagonal cut bristles for drawing straight lines.

Graining brushes These have evenly spaced, coarse bristles for breaking up a glaze into finely spaced stripes for woodgraining. Alternatively, use a dragging or

decorators' brush. *Overgrainers*, with narrow clumps of bristle, are used for adding darker grain and fine details on a dry grained surface.

Mottlers These small brushes have bushy bristles for distressing woodgraining glazes and for adding in highlights. Sizes range from 25-100mm (1-4in).

Softening brushes These come in a range of shapes and sizes and are used to soften brush marks and hard lines. The best ones are made of badger hair and are very expensive. As an alternative, use a dusting brush.

Stencilling brushes These brushes have stiff, tightly packed bristles and a blunt-cut head. They are used to stipple fairly dry paint through a stencil, giving a soft bloom of colour with a crisp edge. Sizes range from 6-50mm (¼-2in) diameter. As an alternative, use a large fitch.

Stippling brushes These stiff-bristled brushes have a flat, square face and are used for removing flecks of glaze, applying speckles of paint and adding texture to thick paint. The best ones are made from badger hair and are very expensive. As an alternative, use a soft, flat-faced brush such as a clothes brush or polishing brush, or use a plastic stippling pad. Sizes range from 75 x 100mm (3 x 4in) to 125 x 175mm (5 x 7in).

Swordliners These brushes have long, tapering bristles and are the best for drawing fine freehand lines. They are used for marbling, lining and detailing. As an alternative, you can use a sable artists' brush or a fitch.

Varnishing brushes Professional decorators use soft, lightweight brushes called *gliders* for brushing out thin varnish evenly, and soft oval-headed brushes for applying thick varnish. Or use a decorators' brush with smooth, dense bristles. Sizes range from 25-75mm (1-3in).

decorators' brush

dragging brush

dusting brush

fantail brush

fitch

mottler

graining brush

lining fitch

varnishing brush

stippling brush

stencilling brush

softening brush

Paint effect tools

Any item for applying paint that isn't a brush is known as a tool. Two familiar tools are paint pads and rollers. More unusual items include combs for making patterns in wet paint and improvised tools such as rags, pads and sponges.

Combs Rubber, plastic wood and metal combs were originally made for woodgraining, but are now used to create a variety of dragged patterns in smooth and textured paint. While the paint is still wet, the comb is pulled across the surface so that the teeth lift off the paint, revealing the contrast colour beneath. For a similar effect use a hair comb or a piece of stifff card with teeth cut at varying intervals in the edge.

comb

Feathers Feathers are the traditional tool for marking the veins in faux marble; long, flexible goose feathers are the choice of professional decorators. Compared to artists' brushes, they give a very natural and ragged effect. You can use the tip of the feather to create fine veining and the edges and face for broader veins.

feathers

Rags Dry rags are used for ragging, rag rolling and colourwashing, and to apply or remove a coloured glaze or wash for a mottled paint effect. The best fabric to use is unglazed cotton – synthetic fabrics don't absorb paint well, and woollen fabrics shed fluff and fibres. Different cotton fabrics, such as sacking, lace and mutton cloth, give their own individual look and texture.

cotton rag

Rollers In addition to standard wool or synthetic paint rollers that give a smooth, even finish, you can buy moulded roller sleeves that create a patterned or textured finish such as stripes, diamonds or bark. *Narrow paint rollers*, designed for painting along skirting boards or behind radiators, are ideal for painting stripes, checks and tartan patterns. Painting a contrasting colour with a long-pile roller over a basecoat produces a cloudy, mottled effect. You can adapt a standard sponge roller by wrapping string around the sleeve to create a textured surface.

Woodgraining tools These tools (sometimes called heartgrainers or rockers) have comb-shaped edges and a textured rubber surface mounted on a curved block. For a straight grain effect the comb is dragged through wet paint, then the curved face of the tool is rocked over the surface to create knot shapes.

Sponges Natural and synthetic sponges are used for sponging on and off. Natural sponges are expensive, but they produce a random texture, essential for techniques like marbling. You can imitate the effect by ripping up a synthetic sponge to give it a more uneven surface. Synthetic sponges have harder edges and produce denser, more regular effects. They can also be carved into shapes for block printing.

mutton cloth

narrow roller

synthetic sponge

natural sponge

woodgraining tool

moulded roller

Care of brushes and tools
Cleaning brushes

Always clean your brushes immediately after use. Never leave them standing in a jar of water or solvent because the bristles will stiffen and bend out of shape. Remove any excess paint from the bristles on a piece of newspaper, then clean off water-based paint in warm running water and solvent-based paint in white (mineral) spirit or brush cleaner. Finish off by washing in warm, soapy water and very gently rubbing the bristles back and forth on the palm of your hand to work the soap into the bristles. Shake out the excess water and smooth the bristles into shape with your fingers. Store small brushes upside down in a jar. Store large brushes flat, or drill a hole through the handle and hang them up. Store a stippling brush bristle-side up.

Cleaning tools

Remove excess paint from the tool as appropriate – wiping, dabbing or rolling it on newspaper. Clean off water-based paint under warm running water and solvent-based paint with white spirit. If removing solvent-based paint from a comb, wipe it off with a rag dampened in white spirit – never soak it in the solvent. Use your hands to squeeze the paint out of a rag, roller or sponge. If necessary, use a scrubbing brush to loosen paint from a comb or woodgrainer. If you are going to dispose of rags or sponges cleaned with white spirit, make sure they are completely dry, as they are flammable.

CRACKLEGLAZING

*Give accessories and wooden furniture a mellow, aged patina
with crackleglaze, a paint or varnishing technique which produces a beautiful,
intricate web of fine cracks over a surface.*

Crackleglazing imitates the subtle, cracked appearance of ageing paint by applying incompatible layers of paint and glaze to the surface. It's a great way of softening the look of newly painted furniture and accessories and makes the contrast with genuinely old pieces less obvious.

You can crackleglaze any item with either paint or varnish. It is best to try it out on small items first, such as gift boxes, wooden picture frames and lamp bases. To get the cracked paint effect, brush a coat of special crackleglaze –

available from home decorating and craft stores – over a basecoat of ordinary emulsion/latex. When the crackleglaze is dry, paint a second colour of emulsion over the top. Within seconds, the top layer begins to crack, revealing the base colour underneath. Experiment with different colour combinations until you get the effect you like.

With varnish, there is no special crackleglaze agent; instead you get a cracked, aged effect by using two layers of incompatible water- and oil- based varnishes.

The crackleglaze technique works well on wood. Tongue-and-groove boards on living or dining room walls make a perfect surface for creating the crackleglaze effect.

THE CRACKLEGLAZE EFFECT

A layer of crackleglaze causes the top coat of emulsion paint to crack instantly as it dries, so it is very important to work quickly or the effect will be ruined. Different brands of crackleglaze require different methods of application – some need to be painted on when tacky, others require a dry surface, so always check the manufacturer's instructions. Paint the top coat over the dried crackleglaze as quickly and lightly as possible, and do not go over the same area twice. To get the desired cracked effect the layers must not mix while wet.

For the most pronounced effect use strong, contrasting colours – red over black for example. If you want to create an impression of antiquity use subdued or muted colours.

YOU WILL NEED

* ❖ **PRIMER** for bare wood or metal
* ❖ **EMULSION PAINT** (LATEX OR ACRYLIC) **in two colours**
* ❖ **12mm (½in) PAINT BRUSHES**
* ❖ **CRACKLEGLAZE**
* ❖ **MATT OR SATIN POLYURETHANE VARNISH**

▶ *Summer-fresh marguerites look perfectly lovely in a heavily crackleglazed wooden plant holder. Here a vivid green base was speedily covered with black paint to give a dramatic crackle effect.*

1 Painting the base colour Make sure the surface is clean, dry and free from grease. Prime bare wood or metal. Apply a coat of emulsion in the first colour over all of the surfaces and leave it to dry.

2 Applying the crackleglaze For an even, squared-effect crackle when the top coat is applied, brush on the crackleglaze in one direction only. For an uneven, crazed effect, brush the glaze on haphazardly. Leave it to dry.

3 Painting the top coat Working quickly, brush on the second emulsion colour, applying it in the opposite direction from the glaze. Apply paint to each section once only, or you will spoil the crackle effect. Leave it to dry.

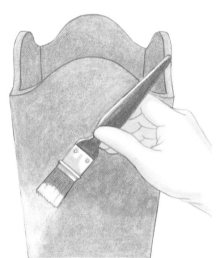

4 Protecting the finish Brush two coats of varnish over the surface, leaving the first to dry before applying the second.

TIP

QUICK RESULTS
Using a hair dryer on a low heat setting speeds up the drying and crackle process. It also causes more pronounced cracks to form.

▶ *Two tones of greeny blue work together here to produce a subtle effect that is perfect for this handy bathroom container.*

CRACKLE VARNISHING

To produce a traditional crackle effect, a quick-drying, water-based varnish is applied over a slower drying oil-based one. The oil-based varnish shrinks as it dries, causing the already hardened water-based varnish on top to break up into cracks. You can accentuate the network of cracks by rubbing some brown artists' oil paint over the surface. The two types of crackle varnish are available from art shops in kit form or separately.

This technique works well on painted or papered surfaces, which makes it a good finish for decoupaged objects such as the table mat illustrated here.

◪ *The crackle varnish effect gives a pleasing, aged finish to a decoupaged surface while simultaneously protecting the design.*

1 Applying first varnish
Brush a thin, even coat of oil-based varnish all over the surface. Allow it to dry until it is just tacky to the touch.

3 Adding colour Thin a little artists' oil paint with oil-based varnish and rub the mixture gently over the whole surface with a cloth, working it well into all the cracks.

2 Applying second varnish
Brush a thick layer of water-based varnish over the top of the oil-based varnish. Leave the varnish to dry. As it dries, cracks will appear.

4 Removing excess colour Use a clean, dry cloth to remove the paint from the surface, leaving just a thin residue in the cracks. Allow the paint to dry for a week before protecting it with two coats of oil-based varnish.

PAINT DISTRESSING

*Distressing is a splendid way to revive wooden furniture
that has deteriorated too far to be restored to its original condition,
or to make a new piece feel a little more at home.*

I n an age when most home furnishings are mass-produced, furniture designs and finishes that are full of character are held in special regard. Nostalgia also plays an important part and, over the years, decorative painters have devised ways of simulating age on painted furniture. These techniques, known as distressing, are easy to master and require little specialist equipment apart from paint brushes and abrasive paper.

The word distressed describes the battered appearance of the furniture rather than any specific techniques used to achieve the look.

In fact, there are a variety of methods you can use, depending on how old you want the piece to appear and which paint you use. Both water- and oil-based paints are suitable for distressing, but use eggshell (flat satin) rather than gloss finish oil paints because their shiny finish is out of keeping with the worn look.

More important than the paint itself is the approach to its application. Remember that you are aiming for a natural look, and understatement is often the key. The more sensitive the handling of the paint, the more convincing the aged quality of the piece will be.

*An old and bruised
kitchen cabinet with a
thick crust of crackled
varnish makes an ideal
starting point for a
distressed paint effect
worked in Prussian
and royal blue paint.*

13

DISTRESSING FURNITURE

All the standard rules of preparing a surface for painting apply to paint distressing. Before applying a base coat and several coats of thinned top coat, untreated wood needs to be primed and painted, while varnished items should be washed thoroughly and sanded down. As you're aiming to simulate layers of paint acquired over several years, don't worry about stripping off existing paint just to replace it.

As long as the item of furniture is structurally sound it doesn't matter how cracked and knocked about it looks – these marks reinforce the time-worn impression. To reproduce the wear and tear of several generations of use, you can even damage the surface of the wood deliberately by knocking it with a bunch of keys or a bag of stones. Evidence of woodworm is a bonus, provided it's been treated and eradicated first. The real enthusiast can even bore fake woodworm holes with a nail or the point of a compass, after applying the final coat of paint.

Once the piece of furniture is prepared, the paint colours must be carefully considered. Two colours are generally used, with the bottom layer of paint showing through in areas that naturally receive the most wear. See page 16 for ideas on selecting paint colours. In the final stages the piece can be given a translucent wash or glaze to mimic the patina of long service.

Depending on which techniques you plan to use, select the tools and materials you need from the list below.

1 Preparing the surface Wash the item thoroughly with warm soapy water to remove dust and dirt and allow to dry. Use a scraper and wire brush to remove any blistered or flaking paint or varnish, then give it a rough sanding to key the surface. Wipe down with a clean cloth.

2 Applying the base coat Apply a coat of primer to new wood and leave to dry. Use a clean paint brush to apply a rough coat of the base colour to the item. Given the casual nature of the distressed finish, don't worry about applying the base coat too thickly or evenly. Allow to dry.

YOU WILL NEED

❖ CLOTHS

❖ SCRAPER, WIRE BRUSH

❖ ABRASIVE PAPER

❖ PAINT BRUSHES

❖ WOOD PRIMER

❖ WATER-BASED EMULSION (LATEX) OR OIL-BASED EGGSHELL (FLAT SATIN) PAINT in two colours

❖ WHITE/MINERAL SPIRIT

❖ COARSE AND MEDIUM-GRADE WIRE WOOL

❖ OLD BUNCH OF KEYS or BAG OF STONES

❖ HAMMER AND CRAFT KNIFE (optional)

❖ NAIL OR PAIR OF COMPASSES (optional)

❖ RAW UMBER AND RAW SIENNA OIL OR ACRYLIC PAINT (optional)

❖ PVA ADHESIVE or TRANSPARENT OIL-BASED GLAZE (optional)

❖ SATIN OR MATT POLYURETHANE VARNISH or FURNITURE WAX

3 Applying the top coat Using an appropriate thinner (water for water-based paint and white spirit for oil-based paint) dilute the top coat paint – one part paint to three parts thinner. Use a clean paint brush to apply two or three thin layers of the top coat paint, allowing each coat to dry before applying the next. Allow to dry thoroughly.

4 Distressing the finish Consider which areas of the item would suffer wear in normal circumstances and use wire wool to rub the paint surface to expose patches of the base coat and bare wood in these areas. On cupboards and chests, concentrate on edges, mouldings and around handles or knobs. On chairs, concentrate on the seat, top back rail and around the base of the legs.

5 Weathering (optional) To give new wood a slightly damaged appearance, beat it with an old bunch of keys or a bag of stones. Use a hammer and craft knife to create small dents and chips. When you are satisfied with the result, wipe down the piece thoroughly. Use a nail or the point of a compass to fake clusters of woodworm holes.

6 Mixing a patina wash/ glaze (optional) Depending on whether you're using water- or oil-based paints, mix equal parts raw umber and raw sienna pigment with water or white spirit to a creamy consistency. Dilute to 15 times its volume with a solution of 7 parts water, 3 parts PVA; or equal parts oil-based glaze and white spirit.

7 **Applying the patina (optional)** Use a small paint brush to apply the patina-effect glaze or wash roughly over one section of the item. With a clean pad of cloth rub the glaze or wash into the surface, removing any excess as you work. Working quickly to keep a wet edge going, continue applying and rubbing the glaze or wash over the remaining sections of the item. Allow to dry completely.

8 **Protecting the surface** Apply a coat of satin or matt clear polyurethane varnish or rub furniture wax over the surface and then buff to a sheen with another soft clean cloth. Repeat the waxing process for extra protection and lustre.

This quaint chair looks as though it has survived generations of family life, yet the same well-worn impression can be created in a few hours by deliberately distressing the paintwork. In this case a sapphire blue top coat is rubbed away to reveal the white base coat and weathered wood underneath.

PAINT COLOURS

The colours of a distressed piece of furniture are as important as the technique itself. It doesn't matter whether you lay down a darker or lighter shade for the base coat but it is important that the colour of the base coat complements the top coat. Subtle colours, which are close to each other in tone, work well, especially mellow, earthy ones. But strong colours can work equally successfully, particularly in a cheerful, Mediterranean-style setting.

Many modern paints tend to be too brash for an antiqued finish; to make them look convincingly old, colours should be softened by adding a small amount of paint in a complementary colour. Mix bright blues with a touch of orange, pinks and reds with green, add a tinge of purple to yellows and vice versa.

Alternatively you can add a small amount of raw umber and/or raw sienna pigment in the form of oil and acrylic paints. These earth colours will tone down any colour and can also be used in a wash or glaze over the top coat to imitate the accumulation of years of patina.

◤ *Muted, natural colours are well suited to the distressed look. Here several coats of paint in softly toning colours have been laid down and then unevenly worn away.*

◀ *Hints of sunshine yellow and patches of bare wood peek through a top coat of jade green, to highlight the outline and carvings of this distinctive chair.*

EMBOSSED EFFECT FRAMES

Give plain picture frames a richly carved look by covering them with self-adhesive relief borders. Highlight the relief pattern with metallic wax for elegant frames which complement all room styles.

Ornately patterned embossed frames draw attention to your pictures and look really special when the relief pattern is highlighted with metallic wax. The technique is easy. You just use a self-adhesive border to cover the frame, then paint it with emulsion (latex or acrylic) to coordinate with the surroundings. When the paint is dry, rub metallic wax over the top and buff to a lustrous finish.

With a self-adhesive border you can create all sorts of embossed effects, from classic key designs to flowing floral-patterned styles. A metallic wax makes the perfect finishing touch. The wax comes in several metallic finishes from rich gold and silver tones to lovely copper, pewter and brass finishes. Both the border and the wax are easy to apply, without the need for special equipment. The border can be bought from large department or do-it-yourself stores; pots of metallic wax are readily available from art and craft shops.

Experiment with a whole range of effects by teaming different base colours with various waxes. For the large frame shown here, gold wax was rubbed over a rust-red emulsion, producing an antique leathery look. On the small frame, the same gilded finish was used over pale blue-green for an aged verdigris effect.

An embossed border, painted with emulsion/latex then finished with gold wax, adds real style to ordinary low-cost picture frames.

HIGHLIGHTING A FRAME

The frame can be made of any smooth, non-absorbent material, such as plastic or sealed wood – choose one with level surrounds so that the border can adhere firmly.

A frame with an ornately moulded or carved finish isn't suitable, but if a mainly plain frame has a narrow moulding you can stick a border over the plain part and paint the uncovered moulding in a coordinating colour.

Borders usually come in three different widths – 6cm (2⅜in), 10cm (4in) and 12.5cm (5in). If your frame is narrower than one of these standard sizes, buy a border with a pattern that lends itself to being trimmed.

1 Cutting the border Measure the width of the border against the frame. If the border is too wide, trim it to fit. If you like, you can leave the border wider than the front of the frame, and wrap the surplus round the sides as shown on the rust-red frame on the previous page.

2 Matching the pattern Cut four lengths of border to fit the sides of the frame, plus an extra pattern repeat at both ends of all four lengths. Roughly match the patterns at each corner, marking in a diagonal mitring line from the inside corner to the outside edge.

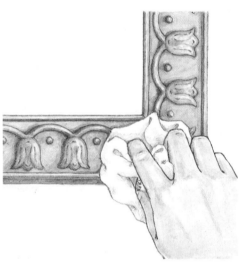

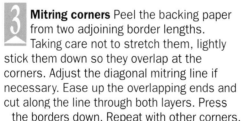

3 Mitring corners Peel the backing paper from two adjoining border lengths. Taking care not to stretch them, lightly stick them down so they overlap at the corners. Adjust the diagonal mitring line if necessary. Ease up the overlapping ends and cut along the line through both layers. Press the borders down. Repeat with other corners.

4 Painting and waxing Apply two coats of emulsion, allowing the paint to dry in between. Using a cloth or the tip of your finger, rub the wax lightly over the pattern, and buff to a soft shine.

GILDING

With the apparent transformation of base items into pure gold or silver, gilding must be the most exclusive and exciting of all decorative effects, and can be less expensive than you might imagine.

Gold is one of man's most treasured raw materials. As such, it is rarely seen in more than small amounts outside the realms of antiquity and royalty. Gilding is the means of over-laying gossamer-fine sheets of gold to give the convincing impression of solid gold. This technique has been employed by master craftsmen for centuries to embellish frames, paint-ings, manuscripts, furniture and architecture, and has broadened to include silver and base metals that simulate gold and silver.

Though for small, quick projects you can use frankly fake gold effects – gold powder, gold wax or gold paint – it's exciting to try your hand at a simplified version of the traditional craft of gilding with metal leaf.

There are two methods of apply-ing metal leaf – water gilding and oil gilding. Water gilding is the more specialist method, involving a painstaking process that requires instruction and considerable practice. A far simpler process, which takes advantage of modern, ready-made preparations and requires few special-ist tools or materials, is oil gilding using metal leaf transfers. This process involves sealing the surface, applying a colouring paste and then a size before adding the transfer leaf.

Once the gilding is complete you can tone the finish to create a softer effect. There are several different ways to add an antique look, including sanding back parts of the leaf and applying finishes, so you can take your newly gilded masterpiece as far back in history as you like.

Overlaid with sheets of ultra-fine metal leaf, these plain café chairs become seats of distinction. A base metal that looks like gold or silver is generally used to cover larger items. On items that will receive a lot of handling and the occasional scuff, apply two or three coats of shellac to protect the delicate leaf.

APPLYING TRANSFER LEAF

As with all types of decoration, it's important to prepare the base thoroughly. Wooden items need to be stripped of any thick paint or varnish and sanded smooth. If necessary punch in nails and fill holes. Remove any rust and flaking paint from a metal surface, then sand smooth and apply a metal primer. Sand plastic to key the surface. Wash plaster and use cellulose filler to repair any chips or cracks.

It's a good idea to practise the technique first on a small item such a photo-frame or candlestick, using less expensive transfer leaf, before using real gold leaf.

All the materials used in gilding are available from specialist art or craft shops or mail-order suppliers.

MATERIALS

At various stages in the gilding process you need to seal the surface using a clear or orange shellac varnish. This is an essential first step if you are gilding a plaster or wood item. Shellac can also be used as a final protective coat. If you seal silver or fake silver with orange shellac the result is silver gilt which looks similar to gold leaf.

Before overlaying the metal leaf you need to apply a special colouring paste known as casein colour. This shows through the metal leaf so you need to select a colour that complements the leaf on top. The traditional colours are red or terracotta under gold; yellow ochre under gold or silver; and blue or grey under aluminium or silver.

To apply the metal leaf to the surface you use oil size, allowing it to dry until it is just tacky. The drying time for different types of size varies from 1–24 hours. Quick-drying size – which takes about an hour to become tacky – is very convenient but needs to be applied in sections when working on a large item, otherwise it becomes too dry to be workable.

Transfer metal leaf comes in sheets of pure gold (or less expensive fake gold, known as Dutch metal) or silver, aluminium and copper. The leaves are backed with wax paper, making them easy to handle, and are sold in books of 25 sheets, each measuring about 8 cm (3⅛in) square. As a rough guide, for a 7.5cm (3in) wide mirror frame, measuring 60 x 90cm (2 x 3ft) you need about three books.

At all stages of the gilding process, work on a covered surface in a well lit room which is dust- and draught-free.

▶ *Although some gilding is highly specialized, even your first attempts can be rewarding. In this case uneven patches of aluminium leaf over a grey undercoat make a simple wooden candlestick look like a really special piece of antique pewter.*

YOU WILL NEED

- ❖ CANDLESTICK or similar item
- ❖ SCRAPS OF WOOD
- ❖ CLEAR SHELLAC
- ❖ STIFF-BRISTLED ARTISTS' BRUSH
- ❖ CASEIN (TEMPERA) COLOUR
- ❖ SOFT-HAIRED ARTISTS' BRUSH
- ❖ FINE GRADE WIRE WOOL
- ❖ CLEAN SHOE POLISHING BRUSH
- ❖ LINT-FREE CLOTH
- ❖ OIL SIZE
- ❖ TRANSFER METAL LEAF
- ❖ SCISSORS (optional)
- ❖ COTTON WOOL BUDS AND BALLS
- ❖ ORANGE SHELLAC (optional)

1 **Preparing the base** Make sure the item to be gilded is sound and its surface smooth and clean. Place it on scraps of wood to raise it off the work surface. Seal wood and plaster with a coat of clear shellac using a hogs' hair brush, and allow to dry.

2 **Applying the casein colour** Dilute the casein with water to the consistency of thick cream. Use a soft-haired brush to apply a coat of casein, washing the brush immediately after use. Allow to dry for two hours then rub lightly with wire wool to remove any brushmarks and runs. Use a shoe polishing brush to buff the surface to a satin finish. Remove any dust. Apply a second coat of casein and finish as before.

3 **Sealing the casein colour** Apply a thin coat of clear shellac with a lint-free cloth. Allow the shellac to dry then rub very gently with fine grade wire wool. Apply a second coat of shellac, allow to dry and rub again with wire wool.

4 **Applying the oil size** Using the oil size directly from its container, apply a coat of size with a soft-haired brush. If you are using quick-drying size on a large item, work on one section of the item at a time. Allow to dry naturally until the size becomes tacky. Use your knuckle to test on an inconspicuous area – when the size is ready it should feel sticky but your hand should come away without leaving a mark.

5 **Placing the metal leaf** Take one transfer leaf from the book. For intricate mouldings use scissors to cut the leaf into smaller, more manageable pieces. Without touching the metal leaf itself, very carefully apply the transfer face down on to the surface.

6 **Removing the backing** Using your fingers, and a cotton wool bud in moulded areas, gently rub the backing paper to press the leaf into place. Slowly peel off the backing, pressing down any leaf that starts to lift off. Continue applying leaf over the remaining sized area, overlapping the edges slightly. If necessary, apply size and leaf to remaining sections.

◹ *Transfer leaf can be used on a variety of surfaces, from a mirror frame to small accessories. A delicate tracery of lines outlining each sheet distinguishes true gilding from fake gold wax, paint or powder.*

7 **Covering bare patches** Use a dry hogs' hair brush to brush away any loose fragments of leaf. If there are bare patches, gild these areas, if necessary re-applying size to the patch. Allow to dry overnight then use cotton wool balls to smooth and polish the leaf.

8 **Distressing and sealing (optional)** Concentrating on the edges and raised areas of the item, which are likely to receive the most wear, very lightly rub the surface of the leaf with wire wool, exposing traces of the colour underneath. If you have used a common metal leaf which tarnishes, or if you think the item will be handled a lot, seal the surface of the leaf with two coats of clear shellac, or orange shellac for a silver-gilt effect.

TONING

Metal leaf, especially Dutch metal and fake silver leaf, can be overly bright when first applied so it is usual to treat the surface to tone down the brashness. Gilders often use special antiquing agents which slightly tarnish the metal, but a more straightforward alternative is to apply a toner. Choose the toner materials according to the type of leaf: real gold and silver are toned with tinted size, common metals with tinted oil glaze. For a slightly duller finish on all types of gilded surface you can dust with rottenstone – a grey polishing powder.

Use artists' water or oil colours to tint the size or oil glaze. The tint colour for gold or silver-gilt is usually raw umber or sepia. To tint aluminium or silver use raw umber and a tiny amount of black. To create a reddish hue tint with burnt sienna. As you become more practised you might want to experiment with other colours – even green and blue – for different effects.

▶ *To emphasize each sheet of gold leaf this mirror frame has been gently polished with a soft cloth against the direction of the overlapping leaves. A delicate rubbing with fine wire wool exposes a little of the surface beneath the gold and a final dusting with rottenstone completes the antique look.*

YOU WILL NEED

Size for gold and silver:
- ❖ PREPARED ARTISTS' SIZE
- ❖ BOWL and JAM JAR
- ❖ ARTISTS' WATERCOLOUR
- ❖ SOFT-HAIRED ARTISTS' BRUSH
- ❖ FINE GRADE WIRE WOOL

Oil glaze for other metals:
- ❖ ARTISTS' OIL COLOUR
- ❖ TURPENTINE
- ❖ BOILED LINSEED OIL
- ❖ SOFT-HAIRED ARTISTS' BRUSH
- ❖ SOFT LINT-FREE CLOTH
- ❖ HOGS' HAIR BRUSH

Rottenstone finish:
- ❖ FURNITURE WAX
- ❖ ROTTENSTONE
- ❖ CLOTH OR NEWSPAPER

TONING REAL GOLD AND SILVER

Applying the size Place the container of prepared size in a bowl of hot water until it melts. In a clean jar dilute a small portion of the size with equal parts warm water. Add to this a small amount of artists' watercolour and mix well. Use a soft artists' brush to apply a thin coat of the size over the gilded surface. Allow to dry, rub lightly with wire wool and apply a second coat. Leave to dry before dusting with rottenstone if desired.

Dusting with rottenstone (optional) At the end of the toning process, after the article has completely dried, use a soft cloth to apply an even coat of furniture wax to the surface. Sprinkle a light dusting of rottenstone on top and leave for about 30 minutes. Use a soft cloth, or wad of newspaper for a slightly tarnished look, to buff the surface, leaving the rottenstone in the crevices and mouldings to create an appropriately antique look.

TONING COMMON METALS

1 Applying oil glaze In a jar, dilute a small amount of artists' oil colour in a little turpentine and use a brush to mix well. Add a few drops of boiled linseed oil and a little more turpentine. Test the glaze on an inconspicuous area of the item to check the colour. Use a soft brush to apply a thin transparent film.

2 Softening the glaze While it is still wet, wipe the glaze with a soft lint-free cloth to distribute the colour and remove some of the glaze. Use a dry, soft-bristled brush to stipple the surface. Allow to dry overnight. Apply wax polish and a dusting of rottenstone if desired.

QUICK GILDING

*Give plain picture frames and other small wooden accessories
a new lease of life with a lustrous mock gilt finish, achieved by applying coats
of coloured metallic powder and wax.*

A gilt finish adds a luxurious, glowing touch to items such as plain wooden picture frames, candlesticks or lamp bases. The traditional method of gilding uses gold leaf, but a less expensive and more convenient way is to use gilt powder and gilt wax or cream to add a colourful gleam. These materials go a long way, the technique isn't difficult and the results are extremely rewarding.

The simplest gilding method is to rub gold wax or cream over the surface of the object being gilded. If you prefer a more colourful finish, try rubbing on a coloured metallic wax or cream. By combining these waxes with different coloured metallic powders you can achieve a wonderful variety of shimmering effects.

Waxes and metallic powders are available from art and craft shops, where you can also buy wax filler sticks and gilt wax crayons for restoring damaged gilded frames and touching up minor surface defects.

Gilding adds a touch of refinement to simple accessories. Here, a gilded candlestick, pedestal shelf and mirror frame set off pretty gold-edged china.

USING GILT POWDER

An effective way of achieving a gilt-style finish is to use gilt powders. The surface is first brushed with gold size – a special kind of varnish to which to the powder adheres. Here gilt powder and coloured wax are combined to gild wooden picture frames, but the technique can be used on many other wood or glass accessories. Before you start, make sure the surface is free of dust and grease. Bare wood needs to be primed with knotting to provide a suitable base for the size.

YOU WILL NEED

❖ MOULDED WOODEN PICTURE FRAME
❖ NEWSPAPER
❖ KNOTTING
❖ Fine-grade SANDPAPER
❖ Small PAINT BRUSH
❖ WATER-BASED GOLD SIZE
❖ GILT POWDER
❖ SAUCER
❖ Small piece of VELVET OR CHAMOIS LEATHER
❖ Spray-on CLEAR POLYURETHANE VARNISH
❖ SOFT CLOTHS
❖ COLOURED METALLIC WAX

1 Preparing the frame Spread sheets of newspaper to protect the work surface. Seal the frame with knotting and rub smooth with fine-grade sandpaper.

2 Applying gold size Using a clean dry paint brush, coat the prepared frame with gold size. Follow the manufacturer's instructions for drying times.

3 Applying gilt powder Pour a little gilt powder on to a saucer. When the gold size is tacky, wrap a small piece of velvet or chamois leather around your index finger and use it to dab gilt powder on to the surface of the frame. If the gold size becomes too dry for the powder to stick, breathe on it to make it tacky again. Cover the whole frame in this way, making sure that you work the powder into the moulding. Leave the frame to dry overnight.

4 Fixing the gilt powder Spray on a coat of clear varnish to fix the gilt powder. Allow to dry.

5 Applying accent colour Using your finger or a soft cloth, rub on coloured metallic wax to the raised part of the frame surfaces. Apply a thin layer for light colour; for a stronger hue apply the wax more densely. When the frame is evenly coated, use a clean soft cloth to buff up a shine, leaving gold in the grooves of the moulding.

◀ The metallic wax is rubbed on once the gilding powder is set and protects the powder from tarnishing. It comes in many vivid shades including, from the top frame, ruby, royal amethyst and emerald.

▼ To gild a frame in powders of two different colours, apply the base colour powder and varnish. Allow to dry, then paint on more size. Add a second shade of powder, blotting it on in cloudy patterns.

▼ You can create a whole range of colourful effects using different combinations of gold size and metallic powder and wax.

metallic powder in Florentine

metallic wax in Aquamarine

metallic powder in Bronze

metallic wax in Royal Amethyst

gold size

ANTIQUE EFFECTS

YOU WILL NEED

❖ WOODEN FRAME
❖ MATT EMULSION/FLAT LATEX PAINT
❖ 2 small PAINT BRUSHES
❖ GOLD SIZE
❖ GILT POWDER
❖ SAUCER
❖ Spray-on clear POLYURETHANE VARNISH
❖ Fine WIRE WOOL, grade 000
❖ CLOTH

For an aged appearance, gilt powder is applied over matt emulsion paint. As the powder does not cover the paint completely, the colour underneath shows through, giving the item a timeworn appearance. Use dark brown or dark red paint for a traditional effect. The antique look can be exaggerated by rubbing away more of the gilt finish with fine wire wool.

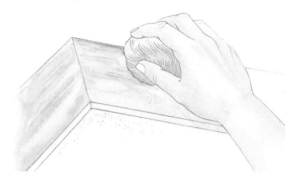

1 **Painting the wood** Prepare bare wood for painting, then apply one or two coats of matt emulsion, allowing each coat to dry.

2 **Gilding the surface** Apply gold size, gilt powder and spray-on varnish to the painted wood as described in steps 1-4 of Gilding a Frame on the previous page.

3 **Distressing the surface** Rub a small piece of fine wire wool over the surface to remove some of the gilt finish. When you are satisfied with the effect wipe away any dust with a damp cloth. Spray on another coat of varnish to protect the surface and allow to dry.

Here, gold size and powder are applied over red paint. Rubbing off some of the gold creates a convincing antique effect.

LIMING WOOD

A highly fashionable yet traditional method of decoration, liming both revitalizes the look of wood and gives it a comforting, time worn appearance.

L iming is a simple technique for bringing out the grain of the wood and giving it a whitened look, as if it has faded naturally over the years – ideal for both restoring old furniture and mellowing new. The soft, textured effect liming produces is especially pleasing in neutral colour schemes.

Liming is most effective on prominently grained woods such as ash, pine and oak. Oak particularly benefits. It is a naturally pale wood that can look rather heavy and dull – all the more so when it is covered in dark varnish, as it often is.

Traditionally, limewash was used for liming wood. However, lime is very caustic so it is safer and just as effective to use liming wax or white eggshell (flat satin) paint, both of which are readily available and easy to apply. Wax produces a particularly subtle effect, with a soft sheen.

For a coloured variation on liming, you can tint the white paint to match a particular colour scheme – or even use a coloured paint for the liming technique. Liming wood that has already been stained a vivid colour is another highly effective option.

Liming gives an attractive, weathered feel to wooden furniture. Use it to tone down the harsh colour of new pine or to give a weather bleached character to dull old pieces.

PREPARING THE WOOD

◪ *This tray was stained to give it an antique look before white paint was wiped over it to soften its appearance.*

Liming can only be applied to clean, bare wood, so you must remove any wax, paint or varnish before you start. You then need to open up the grain of the wood with a wire brush before applying the liming wax or paint, as this improves the final look. Wax can be removed with wire wool and white spirit. Strip paint or varnish from the wood with a commercial liquid, gel or paste stripper. Water-soluble strippers are better than solvent-based ones because they also raise the grain of the wood. Or you can have movable items of furniture stripped of paint and varnish by a commercial dipping service. While this will raise the grain, it may also loosen some of the joints.

Stripping can be a messy business – as can liming with paint – so tackle the whole job out of doors if possible. If you work indoors, spread plenty of old newspapers around to protect the floor, and make sure the room is well ventilated. Indoors or out, wear rubber gloves and old clothes or a large apron.

◪ *White paint lightly tinted with a shade of terracotta was used for the liming on this tray.*

YOU WILL NEED

❖ RUBBER GLOVES
❖ WIRE WOOL 00 grade
❖ WHITE/MINERAL SPIRIT
❖ PAINT/VARNISH STRIPPER
❖ OLD PAINT BRUSH
❖ SCRAPERS AND SHAVEHOOKS
❖ FINE SANDPAPER
❖ STIFF WIRE BRUSH
❖ LINT-FREE COTTON CLOTH

Stripping paint or varnish
Remove any fittings such as knobs and handles, then use a commercial stripper, following the manufacturer's instructions and precautions. Apply liquid or gel with an old paint brush, paste with an old knife. Remove liquids and gels with paint scrapers and shavehooks. Clean the wood as instructed, then rub off any stubborn patches and last traces of paint or varnish with fine sandpaper.

Opening up the grain Brush the wood firmly in the direction of the grain with a stiff wire brush, to open up the grain and remove any soft wood. Wipe away dust with a clean cloth.

TIP

STRIPPING FITTINGS

To strip paint or varnish from metal fittings, tie them together with a piece of string and suspend them in a jar of stripping liquid. Leave them to soak for a few minutes, then take them out and clean them well in white spirit or water, according to instructions.

Liming with Paint

A solvent-based white eggshell/flat satin paint gives wood the classic limewashed look. White is the safest colour, as it goes well with any colour scheme. If you wish to add a hint of colour, however, you can either choose a coloured eggshell paint, or you can mix your own shade using artist's oil colours to tint white eggshell paint. Pale blue-greys and soft pinks are good choices.

Even a small amount of colour has an obvious effect, so be careful not to add too much. Pour a little paint from the tin into a jam jar and experiment with the mixing first.

You Will Need

- Rubber Gloves
- Eggshell/Flat Satin Paint
- Colouring Agents
- Lint-free Cloths
- White/Mineral Spirit
- Wax or Varnish

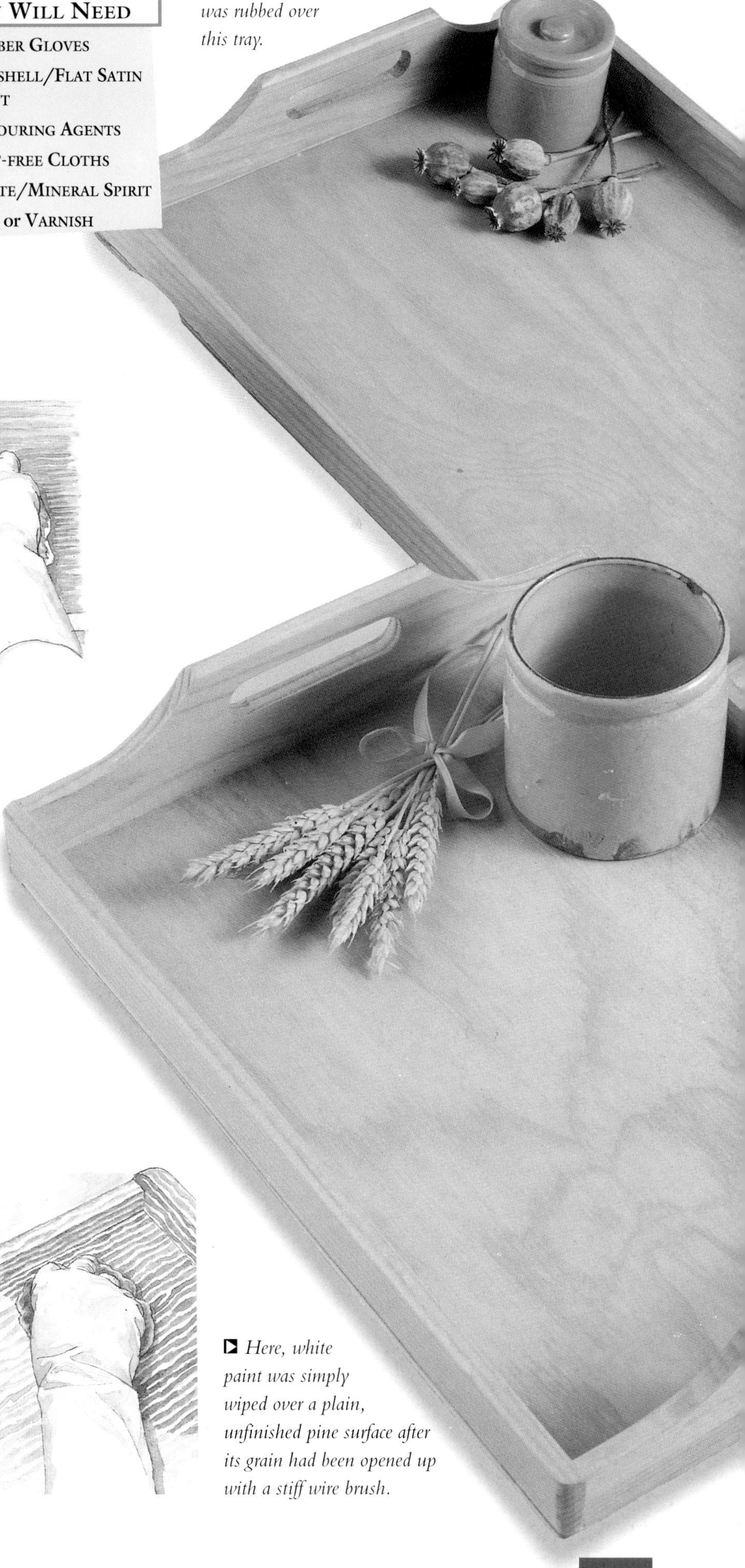

A pale blue-grey tint was used to colour the white paint before it was rubbed over this tray.

Here, white paint was simply wiped over a plain, unfinished pine surface after its grain had been opened up with a stiff wire brush.

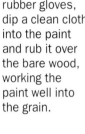

1 Applying the paint Wearing rubber gloves, dip a clean cloth into the paint and rub it over the bare wood, working the paint well into the grain.

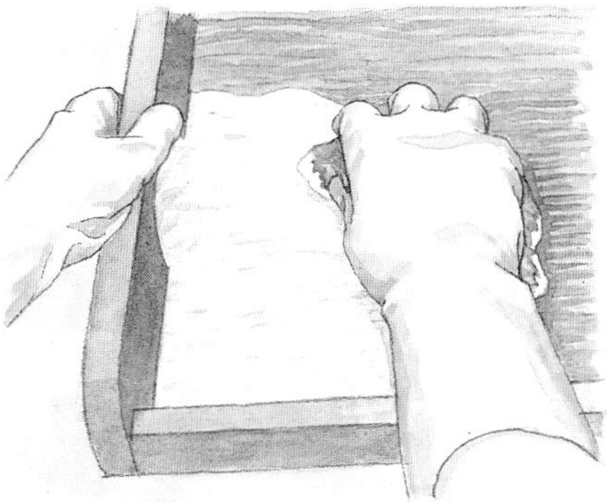

2 Wiping off the paint Dampen a clean cloth with white spirit. Wipe off the excess paint so that colour is left only in the grain. Leave to dry.

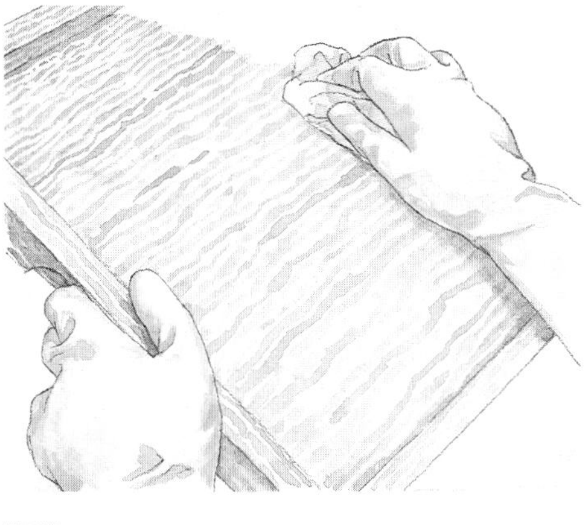

3 Finishing the surface You can leave the wood as it is at this stage. For a more resilient surface with a slight sheen, rub furniture wax all over it with a clean cloth, then buff it up. Or for a hard-wearing finish, apply one or two coats of varnish.

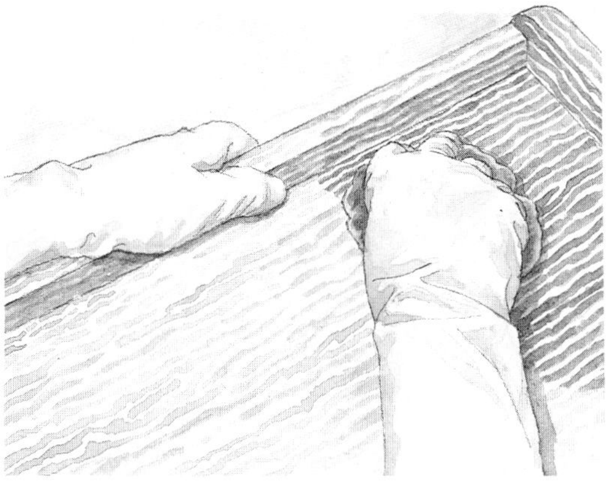

LIMING WITH WAX

Liming wax is available from specialist paint and arts and crafts shops. It gives the wood a slightly more natural bleached appearance with a softer sheen than white eggshell paint.

Protect the limed surface with furniture wax, and wax and polish the wood occasionally to ensure continuous protection.

YOU WILL NEED

- ❖ RUBBER GLOVES
- ❖ FINE STEEL WOOL (000 grade)
- ❖ LIMING WAX
- ❖ FURNITURE WAX
- ❖ LINT-FREE COTTON CLOTH

1 Applying the wax Wearing rubber gloves, pull a piece of steel wool from the roll, form it into a small pad and dip it into the wax. Rub the wax into the wood, working both along and gently across the grain so that every indentation is filled. Change the pad when it becomes clogged. When you have finished, leave the wax to soak for half an hour. The longer you leave it, the more pronounced and grainy the final effect.

2 Polishing off Dip a fresh pad of steel wool into ordinary furniture wax and rub it all over the wood to remove excess liming wax. Buff the wax to a soft shine with a clean cloth.

◪ *For liming smaller items like picture frames and wooden boxes, liming wax is just as easy to work with as paint and produces a gentler effect with a soft sheen.*

MARBLE PAINT EFFECTS

Add a touch of opulence to your home with a paint effect that imitates marble. The subtle colours and delicate veining add real class to projects as diverse as a tiny picture frame or an entire stairwell.

W ith its cool, translucent sheen and delicately veined surface, marble is a very special material – costly to buy, heavy to handle and a challenge to work with. The special qualities of marble have elevated it to the heights of grandeur, so there's always been an interest in simulating the effect with less costly materials like paints and glazes.

Faux (false) marbling can be used on large or small projects, from walls, cornices and skirtings to fireplaces, bath surrounds, pieces of furniture and accessories such as lampbases or picture frames.

To achieve a marble effect, layers of glaze are applied over a base coat, and then the distinctive dark veins are painted in with a fine brush. The characteristic vein formations in

marble are caused by the tremendous pressures which occur during its slow transformation from basic limestone. The variations of colour and stratified patterns are enormous – from cool greys and creams through greens to rich red earthy shades.

To capture the distinctive qualities of marble – its fine tracery of veining and soft cloudiness, colour, pattern and texture – look for inspiration at real examples, such as a pastry slab or tile, or close-up colour pictures of marble. It takes years of practice and skilful use of specialist equipment to achieve a truly authentic effect, especially over large areas; the simple techniques described overleaf give a fantasy marble effect which adds distinction to all sorts of surfaces.

Cool grey marbling adds sophistication to this essentially rustic dining room. When marbling large areas such as a wall, work in sections, or 'blocks' of marble, so that you have time to complete the effect before the paint dries.

MARBLING A FIRE SURROUND

Before you start, practise the marble paint effect on a piece of scrap board. The gradations in colour and intricate tracery of veins mean that mistakes can easily be disguised or blended into the design with a dry brush. Work quickly and lightly so that the effect takes on a fresh, spontaneous quality.

Use your sample or picture of marble as a guide to veining; alternatively, look for marbled paper or a marbling kit that includes veining maps which you can trace off.

PAINTS

You can create convincing marble effects with both water-based and oil-based paints and glazes. Oil-based paints are the traditional choice, and are slow-drying so you have time to build up layers of intense, translucent colour. Modern water-based paints are less messy and almost odour free but they dry rapidly so you need to apply the glazes quickly

and divide a large area into marble 'blocks' which can be worked individually. When marbling a fireplace, work in sections from the mantelshelf down.

The instructions here are for water-based marbling, which is ideal for a first project; once you have gained some expertise, experiment with oil-based paints – apply an eggshell/satin base coat followed by layers of oil-based scumble glaze tinted with artists' oil paint and thinned with white spirit. Both types of paint finish need a top coat of varnish as protection and to create a surface sheen.

The faux marble fire surround shown here has a white emulsion base coat overlaid first with a pale grey and then a dark grey scumble glaze. The fine veins are worked in varying tones of grey and brownish grey. All the glazes are tinted with black and raw umber artists' acrylic paint. Some recipes for other marbling colour combinations are given on page 34.

1 Applying the base coat Cover the surrounding area with newspaper, held in place with masking tape. Ensure the surface is sound, clean and smooth; if necessary apply a coat of the appropriate primer, let dry and sand smooth. Apply two base coats of emulsion to the fireplace, sanding lightly after each coat. Leave to dry.

2 Applying the first glaze In a paint kettle dilute water-based glaze with a little water and mix to a smooth creamy consistency. Gradually add small amounts of the base emulsion colour and artists' acrylic paint to achieve the first glaze colour. Quickly sponge or paint the glaze over one section of the fireplace. While the paint is wet, use a dry sponge or a roll of lint-free cloth to dab away areas of glaze, leaving a mottled effect and revealing about half of the base coat.

3 Adding a second glaze While the first coat is still damp, mix up the second glaze, using more artists' colour to achieve a slightly stronger tint. Sponge on whorls of glaze, lifting some off if necessary, to add pattern and depth. Allow to dry. Repeat the glazing process in sections over the rest of the fireplace and leave to dry.

4 Planning the design With a piece of real marble, pictures of marble or veining maps as guidance, use a soft pencil very lightly to draw a marble veining design on each section of the fireplace. Trail the main veins diagonally across the surface, then add smaller veins branching out from these. Rub out mistakes and soften lines with an eraser.

5 Painting the veins Mix up a little tinted glaze in one of the grey vein colours. Working over one section of the fireplace at a time, hold a fine artists' brush loosely and, with a light, almost shaky touch, paint along some of the marked lines. While the paint is still wet, remove excess by dabbing gently with a sponge or damp cloth. Then further soften the veins by lightly stroking a dry brush or feather over them. Mix up a second grey-brown vein colour and paint in the remaining veins. If necessary emphasize some veins by repainting them.

6 Adding a sheen After the paint effects have thoroughly dried apply an even coat of artists' non-yellowing varnish to protect the surface and provide a sheen like real marble.

▶ *A fireplace surround is an ideal surface for trying out a marble paint effect. Start by painting the mantelshelf and then work on the side pieces to avoid smearing your handiwork.*

MARBLING RECIPES

Marble comes in a wide range of beautiful colours: soft pink and blue, rich red tones and brilliant shades of green streaked with turquoise and gold. You can experiment with different colour effects before you embark on a project – use water-based paints on large sheets of good quality paper and you can use your test pieces as gift wrap. The samples shown here were painted in a base colour, two glazes and two veining colours.

Green marble (1 and 5) Mid-green base coat; glazes in veridian plus burnt umber and in Prussian blue plus black; veining in white and in black. Experiment with quantities to achieve the different effects shown.

Ochre marble (2) Pale yellow base coat; glazes in ochre plus white and in ochre plus raw umber plus white; veining in raw Sienna and in raw umber.

Black marble (3) Black base coat; glazes in white and in Payne's grey plus white; veining in black and in white.

Pink marble (4) Pale pink base coat; glazes in Indian red plus ochre plus white and in crimson red plus ochre plus white; veining in Indian red and in raw umber.

White/grey marble (6) White base coat; glazes in Payne's grey plus white and in Davy's grey plus white; veining in Payne's grey and in black.

T I P
MARBLING IN BLOCKS

If you plan to paint a large area like a stairwell or wall, copy the way marble is traditionally used by dividing the area up into blocks and panels with a pencil and ruler. Each panel can then be painted individually which is easier than trying to paint over a wide expanse. The results give a subtle change in colour and pattern over the whole area, just like genuine marble.

☑ *A marble-effect bath surround is the height of opulence. Use a small natural sponge to apply the glazes quickly over a curved surface like a bath surround. Foam-tipped make-up applicators are useful for adding subtle variations of colour.*

FAUX MARQUETRY

Genuine marquetry is made from shaped pieces of wood veneer. You can create a similar richly patterned faux (false) marquetry effect in glorious warm wood shades using stencils and wood stain over bare wood.

Marquetry is a skilled, decorative craft in which slivers of different coloured wood are cut to shape and inlaid on a wooden base to form intricate geometric patterns or pictorial designs. Since the technique was first practised in the early 17th century, it has been used extensively on small decorative items, fine pieces of furniture and architectural features such as shutters and doors.

The attractive quality of marquetry undoubtedly lies in the delicate graining and glorious colours of natural wood – which range from palest blond, through every shade of rusty red and brown to black ebony. Fine examples of antique marquetry are highly prized and very expensive, but you can obtain a similar effect on a plain wooden surface using wood stains and stencils.

Wood stains are available in a wide range of colours – to match almost every type of real wood. A single dark stain stencilled on bare wood looks very effective, or you can overlay several colours – starting with a pale shade and gradually working up to more intense tones. Rather than applying the stains freehand, stencils are used to provide the clearly defined pattern outlines that are typical of true marquetry designs. For different effects, you can apply the stains directly to the stencils or work a negative stencil using masking fluid to conceal the stencil pattern, then you can stain the non-masked areas.

While many decorative finishes conceal the beauty of wood, this stencilled and stained chest shows how faux marquetry enhances the grain and warm tones unique to real wood.

FAUX MARQUETRY CHEST

You can use the method described below for decorating a wooden chest to transform any plain wooden item into a sumptuous piece of faux marquetry. The results are especially effective on older wooden items but can also add character to a relatively cheap piece of whitewood furniture or to a battered junk store find. Don't be tempted to use it on a genuine antique though, as the wood stain is impossible to remove at a later date.

This brass-bound chest is decorated with negative stencilling, using masking fluid to conceal the blond stencil pattern while a dark stain is applied on top. Choose the colour of the wood stain carefully and always test it on an inconspicuous area of the item first, because it's impossible to lighten the colour once you've applied it. Masking fluid is available from artist's suppliers.

PREPARING THE SURFACE

For faux marquetry, you need to start with a bare wood surface. Remove old polish with methylated spirits and a soft cloth, or an existing paint or varnish with a commercial chemical stripper. If you want a very smooth finish you can use wood filler to fill cracks and holes. To finish, rub lightly along the grain with medium and then fine abrasive paper.

1 Positioning the stencils Decide which stencils you want to use – either work with a ready-made stencil or trace the motifs provided here on to an acetate sheet and cut out the designs with a sharp craft knife or hot knife. Then plan how best to arrange them over the item you are decorating. Make a rough sketch of the stencil arrangement.

2 Stencilling with masking fluid Following your sketch plan of the stencil arrangement, carefully position and attach a stencil to the box with masking tape. Pour a little masking fluid into an old saucer. With a small piece of sponge, dab masking fluid over the cut-out areas of the stencil. Let the masking fluid dry to a shiny, transparent finish.

3 Removing the stencil Remove the masking tape and gently lift off the stencil, taking care not to let the masking fluid peel away. If the masking fluid starts to peel off, carefully trim along the outline of the stencil with a craft knife. Repeat, repositioning the first stencil or using another stencil. Apply masking fluid as before to complete the stencil pattern.

▶ *A mid-oak wood stain contrasts well with the tawny colour of this old pine chest. Don't worry if the item you are decorating isn't in mint condition – signs of age, such as woodworm, add an authentic touch and extensive repairs with wood filler only suggest the item is less valuable.*

4 **Applying the stain** Test the wood stain colour on an inconspicuous area of the box. Use a medium-size brush, sponge or rag to apply wood stain evenly over the outside of the box, first across the wood grain and then along the grain. Repeat until you have the desired depth of colour and leave to dry.

5 **Removing the masking fluid** Rub your fingers or a pencil eraser gently across the surface of the wood to peel off the masking fluid and reveal the negative stencil pattern.

6 **Adding extra colours (optional)** If you want to add any colour highlights, conceal areas you wish to remain the same colour using masking fluid then use an artist's paint brush to apply different colour wood stains over the desired areas. Apply the stain sparingly as it tends to bleed outwards across the wood grain.

7 **Finishing off** When the stain is thoroughly dry, dust the surface and make sure that all traces of masking fluid are removed. Use a soft brush to apply two coats of clear gloss polyurethane varnish to protect the surface. Allow to dry then gently rub the surface in a circular motion with a piece of fine grade wire wool; this dulls the finish to a silky sheen.

STENCIL DESIGNS

Like wallpaper and fabric designs, marquetry reflects the fashions of the time. Restrained linear patterns copied from Ancient Greek and Roman frescoes were popular in the 1750s, whereas only a decade later they were largely superseded by a new vogue for pictorial marquetry, especially of realistically rendered baskets of fruit and flowers framed with interlaced ribbons.

Some popular marquetry patterns are shown here ranging from a Neo-classical Grecian key border to an Art Nouveau inspired rose. You can buy similar designs as ready-made stencils or you can enlarge these outlines on a photocopier and then make an acetate stencil from the enlargement.

As a general rule, you can achieve a stronger decorative effect by selecting simple geometric borders and bold single motifs, rather than attempting to recreate a fine filigree pattern or a complex pictorial scene. As with any faux decorative technique, the trick is to recreate the overall effect of the genuine article, rather than trying to reproduce it in perfect detail.

maypole

Art Nouveau rose

fleur de lys

squares

Celtic knotwork

▶ *This table top illustrates what an effective border pattern you can create by alternating a positive and negative stencil of the same design round the edge.*

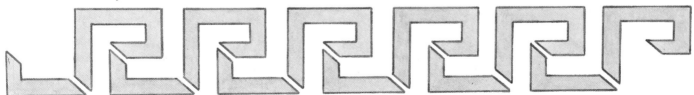

Greek key

STIPPLING

The soft freckles of stippling give a grainy textured finish to furniture and household accessories, and make a subtle background that flatters pictures and furnishings.

Stippling is one of the most delicate paint effects, creating soft, even colours with a subtly mottled appearance. It is a traditional technique for painting walls, wood or metalwork which has been in use since the eighteenth century – prior to the advent of rollers it was one of the best ways to remove any trace of brush marks.

The method for stippling is very similar to ragging off, while the result is a more sophisticated version of sponging. First you apply a light-coloured base coat over the surface and allow it to dry thoroughly. Then brush a thin, oil glaze on top and, while the glaze is still wet, use a flat-faced stippling brush to lift off flecks of the glaze and reveal the colour beneath.

On walls and furniture you can use stippling to create a completely new colour scheme or simply update the existing colour by stippling over the top. Traditionally decorators use a white or pale base with a strong-coloured glaze on top. But you can turn it around and subdue the brashest of base colours by stippling a paler glaze over it. There are no hard and fast rules. Experiment with contrasting or toning colours to create the exact colour combination you want. However, avoid using two very pale or closely related colours as the delicate effect of stippling is lost.

The classic colours of stippling combine a pale base coat with a deeper toning stipple on top. Here a background of primrose yellow stippled with an apricot glaze creates a golden blush of colour on both the walls and candlestick lampstands.

STIPPLING WALLS

Achieving a uniform finish with stippling is quite time consuming, so if possible get someone to help you. Then you can develop a working pattern – one person brushing on the glaze and the other stippling it off.

Make sure the surface you plan to work on is in good condition before you start, as the finish tends to highlight imperfections.

STIPPLING TOOLS

Stippling brushes are flat-faced, usually square and have thick, soft bristles which produce a very fine and even stipple. They are often made from badgers' hair which has split ends that hold the glaze. Although they are fairly expensive, if you are stippling a large area they are a worthwhile investment. For a smaller wall or a piece of furniture you may want to use a cheaper substitute. Try a dusting brush, shoe brush, soft hair brush, even a broom as long as the bristles are all the same length – otherwise just trim them level with sharp scissors. Plastic stippling pads, available from do-it-yourself stores, are another inexpensive option, though the effect they create is very coarse – quite dissimilar to that of a brush.

If you want to use a proper stippling brush, buy an 18 x 12cm (7 x 5in), or larger, brush for walls; an 8 x 10cm (3 x 4in) brush for furniture; and a 10 x 2.5cm (4 x 1in) brush for corners and small areas.

A quicker alternative to stippling with a brush is to use a fluffy-head roller, made from lambswool or mohair, or a coarse polystyrene roller. However the results are more blotchy than when using a brush – closer to the open texture of ragging and sponging – and the roller is more likely to skid.

PAINTS

For the base coat use an oil-based paint (also known as solvent-based paint), such as eggshell, and for the stippling use an oil-based glaze. The oil-based glaze stays wet longer so you have time to work it, and it also makes it easier to keep a wet edge going.

To make the glaze you need to mix together transparent oil glaze (also known as scumble glaze), white spirit as a thinner, and artists' oil paint to colour the glaze. To lighten the tone, or stop yellowing, you can also add a small amount of white eggshell paint, but take care you don't add too much as it makes the glaze dry more quickly.

Make sure you mix up enough glaze for the entire project, because it is difficult to colour match another batch. Two litres (3.5 pints) of glaze are sufficient to stipple the walls of a room measuring 4.5m (15ft) square. As you go through the process of stippling, test each stage on a piece of scrap paper to make sure the glaze is the right colour and to practise your stippling technique.

YOU WILL NEED

- ❖ DUST SHEETS
- ❖ EGGSHELL/FLAT SATIN BASE PAINT
- ❖ PAINT ROLLER, TRAY
- ❖ PAINT KETTLE/SMALL BASIN
- ❖ TRANSPARENT OIL-BASED (SCUMBLE) GLAZE
- ❖ WHITE/MINERAL SPIRIT
- ❖ CLEAN JAM JAR
- ❖ ARTISTS' OIL COLOURS
- ❖ PALETTE KNIFE
- ❖ 100-150mm (4-6in) PAINT BRUSH
- ❖ STIPPLING BRUSH
- ❖ MATT OR SATIN CLEAR POLYURETHANE VARNISH

1 Painting the base coat Cover the floor and any nearby furniture with dust sheets to protect them. Check that the walls are sound and clean. Fill any cracks and holes, and sand smooth any rough areas. Use a roller to paint the walls with a base coat of eggshell. Apply a second coat if necessary, allowing each coat to dry thoroughly.

2 Mixing the oil glaze In a paint kettle mix equal parts transparent oil-based glaze and white spirit. Squeeze a little artists' oil paint into a jam jar and add a small amount of white spirit to thin it. Use a palette knife to mix it. If desired, blend in a little white eggshell paint. Gradually add the paint to the glaze and stir it in well. If necessary add more thinned paint to the desired shade.

Stippling an intense pansy-purple oil glaze over a base coat in a paler shade of purple creates a rich depth of colour. The two-tone effect is further highlighted by using a heavyweight stippling brush with plastic bristles.

3 Applying the glaze Start in the corner of a window wall or other inconspicuous area. Use a paint brush to apply a thin, even film of glaze in a vertical strip about 60cm (2ft) wide. The glaze should be thin enough for brush marks to be visible and the base coat to show through.

4 Stippling the glaze Start at the top of the strip while the glaze is still wet. Hold the stippling brush square on to the wall and strike the glaze lightly but firmly with the bristles. Continue stippling evenly over the wall. If the brush skids, paint and stipple again. Remove any build up of glaze on the brush by dabbing it on dry paper – don't use white spirit as it may cause runs across the glaze. Use a small brush in edges and corners and, if there is a build up of paint, wait until the glaze is almost dry before taking it out with a small brush.

5 Checking the effect
Stand back from the wall at intervals to check the result. If necessary, lighten denser patches by further stippling and darken paler patches by picking up a touch of glaze on the bristles and stippling on the glaze.

6 Completing the stippling Continue working in strips along the wall, taking care to stipple the joins between the strips. Stipple one entire wall at a time – if you allow the glaze to dry midway it leaves a mark. Once you have stippled one wall continue on the opposite wall, before coming back to tackle the adjacent wall, otherwise you may smear the glaze on the adjacent wall. Allow the glaze to dry thoroughly.

7 Varnishing (optional) If you are likely to wash the walls occasionally, protect the finish with clear varnish. Apply two coats of matt or satin varnish, allowing each coat to dry. Varnish darkens the colour of the paint very slightly, emphasizing the stippled effect.

TIP

CHANGING COLOURS

If you're tired of the paint colour on your walls, rather than starting from scratch you could clean the surface and stipple on top. Subdue an overpowering colour by stippling a paler shade or jazz up a dull finish with a bright new colour.

❖

Oil glaze tends to yellow in heat so don't use it on radiators or hot pipes. Yellowing also occurs with lack of sunlight, so expect a masked area – for example behind a picture – to discolour. You can add a small amount of white eggshell paint to the glaze to reduce yellowing.

COLOUR COMBINATIONS

Working with oil glaze paint that you mix up yourself – to whatever colours you choose – means you can concoct a unique colour palette and achieve exactly the desired shade. You can add a little more of the same colour to deepen the hue, a dash of white eggshell to tone it down slightly, or turn to a completely different tube of paint to create a whole new shade. Because you apply the glaze in a thin film and the stippling process removes some of the glaze, the colour of the base coat also affects the stippled look. A brighter or darker base coat livens up a softer glaze stippled on top, while a pale base coat calms a very vivid glaze.

The best way to make sure you get exactly the right colour combination is to do colour tests on sheets of scrap paper. If you are intending to stipple a wall, tape the test pieces on to it so you can check the effect under the appropriate light.

◀ *Mix together lavender blue with stipples of sweet violet to create a dappled lilac finish.*

▼ *Blend muted pistachio with freckles of rich malachite and you generate a lively frosty green.*

◀ *A pale pink background stippled over with a crushed raspberry glaze creates a soft blush of old rose.*

VERDIGRIS PAINT EFFECTS

Over the years, copper slowly weathers, turning a beautiful blue-green colour. You can create a similar antique patina in a couple of hours with a little sleight of hand and a few pots of paint.

The word verdigris comes from the old French *verd de Grèce*, meaning green of Greece. This was the name of a copper pigment used to make green paint about 2000 years ago. Today the word verdigris is more commonly used to describe the green, powdery corrosion of any metal with a high copper content, when it is exposed to air and water for a long time. This natural patination has a rich subtlety which hints at antiquity without being ostentatious. Its appeal is such that metalworkers and artists have developed techniques to reproduce the effect.

The easiest way to create a surprisingly authentic verdigris effect is with paint. By stippling different shades of blue-green, one on top of the other, you can create a soft bloom of colour that closely mimics the real thing. Natural verdigris can vary from a chalky turquoise to a brilliant emerald green, so you can adjust the paint colours slightly, to blend with your own colour scheme, and still keep them authentic.

When choosing an item to decorate, remember that natural verdigris occurs on metal, so it would be unrealistic to use it on some other materials, such as wood. But the technique is ideal for adding an aged character to low cost items – you can turn a plastic planter, for example, into an antique-effect bronze urn or a mass produced garden statue into an original looking figurine. Protect items for the garden with two or three coats of polyurethane varnish.

Give new garden furniture a softly weathered look decorated with a verdigris paint effect. The dappled shades of pale green and turquoise look especially pretty in a conservatory or garden setting.

BASIC VERDIGRIS PAINT EFFECTS

Artists' acrylic paints are ideal for verdigris effects, being easy to work with and quick drying – whether sponged or stippled, they are dry to the touch in moments. The recipe for a basic verdigris paint effect requires four shades of acrylic paint: burnt umber for the base coat, and two shades of green plus white.

Artists' acrylics are sold in tubes or pots and, for all but the largest projects, a small pot or tube of each is adequate. Alternatively, you can buy a kit which includes all the paint colours ready mixed, a stippling brush and sometimes a metallic wax crayon for highlighting. Kits are available at art and craft stores.

To apply the paint, use either a stippling brush or small pieces of sponge. You may find a sponge is better for painting intricate items, such as the wire basket shown here, because the bristles of a brush would enclose around the strips of wire, losing the stippled effect. Experiment on a piece of scrap paper or the underside of the item, to test the paint colours and the most effective way to apply them, looking at examples or pictures of genuine copper verdigris for a colour match. Vary the thickness of the paint for a slightly textured effect.

For really convincing results you can embellish the basic verdigris effect with texture or colour highlights; techniques for these are described on page 46.

PAINTING LARGE ITEMS

For larger items, such as garden furniture, you may find it's more economical to use tester pots of matt emulsion paint (flat latex) rather than artists' acrylic. Most large do-it-yourself stores offer a paint-mixing service so you should be able to get appropriate colours for different verdigris effects.

With a paint or stippling brush, take up a small amount of paint and stipple it firmly using only the tips of the bristles. Dab the brush on a pad of newspaper fairly frequently to prevent the bristles becoming clogged.

1 Preparing the surface Remove any spots of rust or flaking paint on a metal surface with a wire brush. Rub plastic with wet and dry abrasive paper to key the surface. Use a rag and white spirit to remove any grease, then use a small paint brush to apply rust-resistant primer to metal items, or all-purpose primer to plastic. Allow to dry.

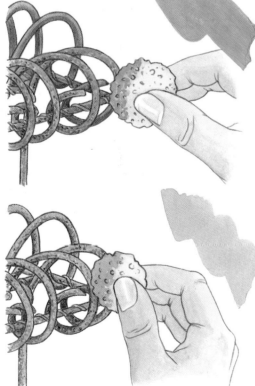

2 Applying the base coat Dilute a little burnt umber acrylic paint with a small amount of water on a saucer. Then either brush or sponge the paint all over the surface to create a smooth, matt base colour. Leave to dry thoroughly.

3 Stippling the first colour On a saucer, mix turquoise green and white acrylic paint to produce a pale blue-green colour. Use a clean piece of sponge to dab the paint lightly over the surface, leaving random patches of base colour showing through. If the sponge becomes clogged, use a fresh, dry piece.

4 Stippling the second colour Mix together white and emerald green paint to produce a pale mint green colour and use a clean piece of sponge to apply as before. If desired, follow the techniques on page 46 to add further highlights.

5 Finishing off To weather proof the verdigris effect for articles to be left outdoors, finish with two or three coats of clear matt polyurethane varnish, letting each coat dry before the next application.

▶ *Part of the art of faux verdigris is applying paint in subtle drifts of colour in order to achieve a natural looking finish. Look at real examples, then mix your paint colours to match.*

◀ *For a powdery look, stipple or sponge the layers of green paint using a very dry brush or sponge and allow the underlying colours to show through.*

SPECIAL EFFECTS

Real verdigris varies considerably in colour and texture depending on how it has weathered and its metal composition. The basic method shown on the previous pages gives a typical verdigris look but for a really authentic finish you can also add texture and colour highlights. Corrosion may give the surface a slightly pitted finish or produce a white chalky residue; it might also produce tinges of yellow or a glimmer of the base metal. Select a special effect to add interest to your chosen object: smooth plastic, for example, will look more authentic if a rougher texture is added with sand. Select the appropriate materials from the list, right, for the effect you wish to produce.

YOU WILL NEED

❖ SAND

❖ FINE GRADE WIRE WOOL

❖ YELLOW OCHRE SPRAY PAINT

❖ PLASTER CASTING POWDER

❖ COPPER or BRONZE METALLIC WAX

For a more realistic verdigris effect you can add both textural and colour highlights. To achieve the pitted, bronze finish that transforms this plastic planter, sprinkle a handful of sand over the wet primer before applying the verdigris colours, then add a touch of bronze metallic wax after the final coat of varnish.

Creating texture Immediately after applying a coat of primer, sprinkle the surface with sand. Allow to dry, then apply the basic verdigris colours described previously.

Distressing the surface After applying the basic verdigris colours, use a piece of fine grade wire wool to rub the surface lightly, revealing patches of the burnt umber base coat underneath. Take care not to remove any of the underlying primer.

Adding yellow highlights To add a slightly yellow tinge to the verdigris, apply haphazard patches of yellow ochre spray paint on top of the basic verdigris colours. Holding the can at an angle about 25cm (10in) from the surface, deliver the paint in single short bursts that lightly dust the surface.

Dusting with plaster powder Use the tips of your fingers to flick droplets of water over the basic verdigris finish then, while still wet, sprinkle with a light dusting of plaster casting powder. Press the powder into the wet areas, concentrating on the crevices. Knock or brush off any excess powder.

Adding metallic highlights After applying varnish to seal the surface, use your fingertip to rub copper or bronze metallic wax sparingly over small areas of the surface, concentrating on any raised areas.

WOODGRAINING

A way of painting a wood-effect finish on to most plain smooth surfaces, woodgraining is pure artifice. It's a particularly effective way to add character to small areas, such as cupboard doors or panelling.

W oodgraining has been used by craftsmen for centuries to imitate the beautiful pattern and rich, warm hues of natural wood. In the 19th century, decorators jealously guarded the secrets of their paint recipes and spent years perfecting techniques with combs, quills and feathers. As a beginner you can't expect to achieve perfect reproductions of the genuine article, but with modern tools and materials you can easily create a range of handsome effects to capture some of the quality of natural wood.

In woodgraining, it's usually best to keep the base coat several tones lighter than the glaze. You can work either in glowing real-wood tones – perhaps to match a new piece of furniture with older items in a room – or in other shades, such as Colonial American blue, to imitate old painted wood or for sheer fantasy effects.

Stick to the simple techniques described overleaf at first, and before you begin spend plenty of time practising with different grain and colour effects. Your first efforts and any mistakes can be simply brushed out or wiped off. As your skills develop, try your hand at creating knots, whorls and burrs, or the figured graining of heartwood, to simulate the look of real wood, from cosy pine to exotic mahogany.

A three-in-one rocker tool and a water-based scumble glaze tinted with emulsion paint are used for the techniques described overleaf. Most flat, smooth woods, MDF (medium density fibreboard) or similar are suitable surfaces. Don't try to woodgrain a laminated or intricately worked finish, or a large expanse of wall unless it's panelled.

A white glaze woodgrained over a honey-coloured base gives a light, modern effect – if woodgraining for a panelled effect, mark the edges of the 'planks' first with a plumb line to help keep your graining vertical.

WOODGRAINING TECHNIQUES

A special plastic graining rocker with a comb edge, available from do-it-yourself stores, is a useful little tool for simulating straight and quarter-sawn grain, and a swirling effect that looks like heartwood. If you're covering a large area it may be worth investing in a wider, flexible rubber graining tool, available from specialist paint shops and used by professionals for heart graining and other special effects. Flexible graining combs with different teeth spacings are also available. An artist's stiff-bristled paint brush may be useful for a grain effect on panel mouldings, and a small, soft paint brush is handy for softening the final effect and touching up. Wipe clean all the graining tools after each run, so that they don't become clogged with paint.

TYPES OF GLAZE

Scumble glazes are available in a water or oil base. The effect shown here is created using a water-based glaze, which is easy to work with and odour free. It can be bought ready tinted or, for a wider choice of colour, you can use a clear scumble glaze that's specially formulated to be mixed with matt emulsion paint.

Follow the manufacturer's instructions for mixing rates and drying times – most water-based glazes dry in about one hour, so make sure you can work fairly quickly without delay by having close at hand all your tools and equipment, plus a bucket of clean water and a cloth to wipe off any mistakes or splashes.

1 Painting the base coat Make sure surfaces are clean and sanded smooth. Use a household paint brush to apply two coats of eggshell paint over the entire surface and leave to dry. Lightly sand smooth. If necessary, mix four parts water-based scumble glaze with one part matt emulsion paint, or as recommended on the label.

2 Applying the scumble glaze Working quickly in line with the intended grain effect, use the household paint brush to apply the scumble glaze to a manageable section – about 1sq m/yd – of the surface. Work the paint in well on any panel moulding, finishing with brush strokes along the line of the intended grain.

3 Combing straight grain Using the comb edge of the rocker graining tool, comb on a straight grain effect by drawing the tool firmly over the surface in strips in the direction of the intended grain. To create subtle variations, try altering the pressure on the teeth – light for fine grain, heavier for coarse – or introduce a slight wave effect.

4 Combing special effects (optional) Change the position of the detachable handle on the rocker graining tool and lightly use the notched edge to make a few wavy diagonal marks for a quartersawn oak effect; or use the notched edge straight to create a wider grain effect.

5 **Adding heart grain** Gently but firmly, and still working with the grain, pull the tilted face of the rocker over some of the grained strips, rocking it in a smooth, continuous motion to create heart grain effects.

6 **Completing the graining** If necessary soften the effect with a fine paint brush or small cloth pad. Touch up the edges with a comb or paint brush. Repeat the steps to woodgrain the rest of the surface in sections. Leave the surface to dry completely then seal with polyurethane varnish.

◿ *Rather than trying to create an authentic bare wood effect, for a first project try experimenting with a colour such as this lilac for a fantasy finish or to capture the bleached look of old painted wood.*

TIP
FOLLOW THE GRAIN
To capture the natural charm of wood, base your graining on a real sample – perhaps a wooden tray or small piece of furniture, or a clear photograph. Pine is a good choice for a first project. Study the patterns and graining carefully, and have your sample near you to refer to while you work.

WOOD EFFECTS

Once you've mastered the basic woodgraining technique given on the previous pages, you may want to brush up your skills and experiment with more authentic wood effects using a variety of tools including combs, specialist figured and straight graining tools, brushes, sponges and cloths. Skilled grainers also use special brushes such as a spalter, but you can improvise by using a good quality paint brush.

The first step always is to study the patterns, graining and colour of actual wood.

Every type of wood has its own pattern, and the part of the log from which the wood is cut also affects the graining. The outer rings (sapwood) are usually straight grained. The centre of the log, the heartwood, has figured graining, sometimes around a knot. Burrs are the result of wood cut from growths on the trunk.

Experiment on small projects to develop your skills; though the art of woodgraining takes years to perfect, with practice you can achieve very pleasing results.

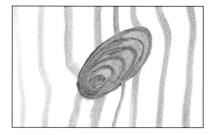
▷ *The effect created by different cuts of wood – in this case pine – works well on this bath, with 'planks' of figured heartwood in the panels and straight-grained sapwood on the frame.*

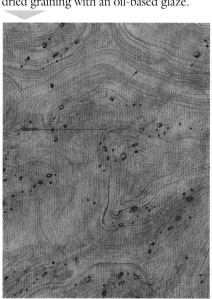

Pine With its clearly defined straight grain on the outer rings and figured heartwood from the centre of the log, pine is one of the most common and easily recognizable woods. It's also the simplest to copy. Use a rocker tool or special combs and graining tools. Knots can be painted on by hand.

Oak Another common wood, oak has straight graining which is more even and closer spaced than pine, and the heartwood figuring is less pronounced. Fine wavy close-graining can be added with a comb. Oak is often cut in quarters (quartersawn) which creates short wavy diagonal marks – add these after the straight and wavy graining with a piece of cloth wrapped around a finger. Use a wooden toothpick or the edge of a cork to add small burrs, or to sharpen and redefine any of the straight graining that has become blurred.

Burred wood Many trees, such as walnut and elm, produce burred wood, with its fine veining and flowing swirls. The technique is tricky, so work on small projects. Create swirling by turning a sponge over a very wet glaze. Faint horizontal marks are painted with a wide spalter or good quality paint brush. A fine brush is used for painting in small oval burrs, and a brush called a pencil dragger, or a fine brush, to add veins – these wavy rounded lines follow the sponge patterns. For a rich effect, paint the dried graining with an oil-based glaze.

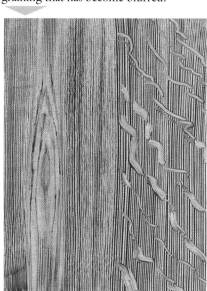

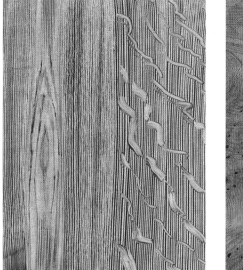

STENCILLING ON WOOD

*Stencilled designs add originality and charm to plain wooden items.
Choose from a wide range of motifs, add your own choice of colour and
have fun experimenting with different creative effects.*

Pre-cut stencils are readily available, inexpensive decorating tools that you can use on almost any item of wooden furniture. A stencilled design can make a junk shop find look really special, or adds an individual touch to mass produced modern pieces. Tables, chairs, headboards, drawers and cupboard doors are all ideal candidates for an individual stencilled motif.

Work on a flat surface to begin with – move on to curved surfaces when you get the hang of the technique. Bold designs without too much detail are the easiest to work with. Stick to a simple shape and a few basic colours to start. Luckily, the charm of stencilling is its simple hand-done look so it doesn't matter if you make a small mistake.

Once you are familiar with the technique, you can start rearranging various parts of a motif to create your own different designs.

A small trug like this makes an ideal first-time stencilling project – you practise the technique and get charming results at the same time.

CHOOSING THE DESIGN

Always consider how the stencil design relates to the shape of the furniture to be stencilled. A round table, chair seat or square cupboard door are all suited to a circular design. For a rectangular table or cupboard door, choose an oblong-shaped motif for the centre, or a trailing floral design as a border. For straight sided table and chair legs or the shelf edges in a bookcase, try a border design which can be repeated along the length as needed. You can buy special corner stencils for continuing the design round bends.

POSITIONING MOTIFS

To decide on the best places for your motif, prepare a test piece on plain paper. Cut it out and tape it to the piece of furniture in different posi-

tions until you're happy with the arrangement. At the same time experiment with isolating separate parts of the motif for use on smaller areas like chair backs or table legs.

PREPARING WOOD

Make sure the surface is clean, dry and sound. You can stencil straight on to smooth, untreated wood but if it is a bit rough sand it down lightly with fine glasspaper. Painted or varnished areas also need a light sanding to key the surface. Wipe away a waxed finish with a little white/mineral spirit.

Use stencil paints which are easy to apply, fast-drying and come in a good range of colours. Forest green, fiery red, electric blue and white were used on this corner cupboard.

HOW TO STENCIL

1 Fixing the stencil Gently press out the cut-out sections of the stencil. Carefully position and attach it to the surface with masking tape. Decide which part of the stencil to colour first, and mask off adjoining, different coloured sections with strips of masking tape.

2 Picking up paint Moisten the sponge lightly with water. Pour some paint into the saucer. Dip a corner of the sponge into the paint and dab off most of it on scrap paper, so that the sponge is almost dry.

3 Applying the paint Dab the sponge on to the exposed cut-out areas of the stencil, making sure that the paint goes right up to the edges. To darken the colour, go over the same cut-out areas with the sponge again. Leave to dry. When you've finished using the first colour, wash the sponge and saucer ready for the second.

4 Adding another colour Ease the masking tape away from the areas to be painted in the second colour. Mask off adjoining areas and paint the second colour in exactly the same way as the first. Repeat this step for the third and fourth colours.

◀ *Stencilled tulips bring a touch of spring to a corner cupboard. You can use one of the colours to highlight other features — here red provides a bright frame for the stencil design.*

MORE FROM YOUR STENCIL

Take small coordinating designs from the one stencil by masking off the main motif and using the remaining part as a separate stencil. You may find it easier to cut away the part you want to use.

Flip a stencil over to vary the design, or to produce a symmetrical design. For a mirror image, lightly mark the centre points between the motifs to ensure accurate positioning when the stencil is turned over.

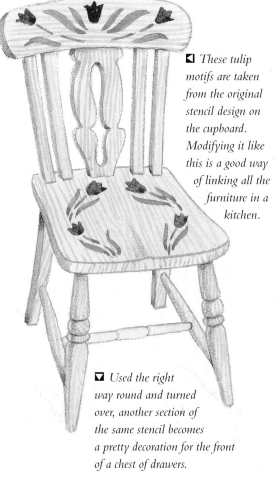

◀ *These tulip motifs are taken from the original stencil design on the cupboard. Modifying it like this is a good way of linking all the furniture in a kitchen.*

◀ *Used the right way round and turned over, another section of the same stencil becomes a pretty decoration for the front of a chest of drawers.*

5 **Cleaning up** When all the paint is dry, carefully peel off the masking tape and remove the stencil. Wash stencil, sponge and saucer under the tap after use.

6 **Protecting the design** Brush on two coats of clear polyurethane varnish, allowing each to dry before sanding down lightly with fine glasspaper between the coats.

53

SHADING AND HIGHLIGHTING

Stencilled motifs often look more effective when they are shaded with a second colour over certain areas. For the best effect, use two shades of the same colour – a dark shade over a light one to suggest shadow, a lighter shade on a dark one for highlights. Apply the paint lightly and wait until the first colour is dry before applying the next.

Practise shading on a piece of scrap paper first to get a feel for the effect. You will soon be able to achieve quite subtle gradations of colour by fading out the second shade as you work across the area. If necessary, you can also remove a little paint by dabbing with a slightly damp, clean sponge to soften the effect.

▶ *Stencilled patterns are often inspired by their surroundings. Here, stencilling an ivy leaf design on to the wooden tabletop matches it perfectly to the tea set.*

Applying shading Dip bristle tips into the second colour and dab off excess. For a shadow effect, apply a darker shade down one side of each cut-out shape. Work from the outside into the centre, leaving more colour at the edge. Dab sparingly so that some of the first colour shows through. For highlights, use the brush in the same way to apply a light colour down the opposite side.

▶ *When you compare the trail of stencilled ivy on this trug with the one on the first page, you will see what a difference a little shading and highlighting can make, even to a simple, one colour motif.*

CREATING A STENCIL

Use a motif printed on fabric or wallpaper as the starting point for creating your own stencil – it's a clever way of linking the existing furnishings in a room to new curtains, bedlinen or wallcovering.

Designing and making your own stencil is easy when you adapt it from a fabric print or wallpaper design. If the room is already decorated, making your own stencil enables you to create innovative designs that match and enhance the original fabric, as well as brightening up the room. Or, if you're decorating a room from scratch, knowing how to make your own stencil means you are not restricted to mass-produced designs, but can create your own unique patterns.

Choose a pattern like the colourful wild animal print shown here, with well defined motifs and flat areas of colour for your first project. All you need do is trace off a motif you want and perhaps enlarge or reduce it to fit. Then you copy the various colour areas on to separate sheets of acetate and cut them out.

If the motif is more complicated, you still start by tracing it – then simplify or strengthen the design lines to make a workable stencil. You can modify the arrangement of a motif to your own specifications too. The dainty flowers on the cupboard drawers shown above, for example, are taken from the fabric print but arranged in a different way to create a more balanced, symmetrical motif.

The bright, bold animal shapes on this nursery curtain fabric make ideal motifs for stencils. Use them to decorate furniture, accessories and even as a chair-rail frieze for a unique, coordinated room scheme.

PREPARING THE DESIGN

Take time to select the motif you are going to stencil and to consider how to position it on the item. With small accessories, such as a lampshade, one bold motif may be all that is needed; with larger items of furniture (or even walls) you may need to group a few motifs together to achieve a strong composition.

If you are using more than one motif there are some tricks you can employ to make your design more interesting. Try repeating a single motif but reversing its direction so, for instance, two animals face each other. Alternatively, look for smaller motifs within the source pattern that can be used as fillers or to add detail to a main motif. You will soon discover that there is no reason for sticking rigidly to the source pattern – doubling up, re-ordering or combining different parts of

the pattern into a new grouping often makes a more effective stencil design than just copying the original pattern exactly.

For some designs you only need to cut one stencil – either they are a single colour design or it is easy to mask off the different colours. When the motif is slightly larger or more complicated, it is quicker to cut a separate stencil for each colour rather than having a single stencil and masking off numerous cut-out areas.

Acetate sheet is best for making the stencil. As it is clear, you can see the colours already stencilled underneath and use them for accurately aligning or registering the stencil for the second and subsequent colours. Sheets of acetate and other equipment for cutting stencils are available from craft, DIY and specialist stencil stores.

YOU WILL NEED

❖ SUITABLE MOTIF
❖ TRACING PAPER
❖ COLOURED PENCILS
❖ SOFT LEAD PENCIL
❖ CUTTING MAT
❖ MASKING TAPE
❖ SHEETS OF CLEAR ACETATE FILM
❖ FINE PERMANENT FELT-TIP PEN
❖ CRAFT KNIFE

1 Tracing the motif If copying the motif directly from fabric, stretch the appropriate area out flat on a firm surface. Position the tracing paper on top, securing it with masking tape. Draw around the outer edge of the motif, then trace around any different areas of colour. Do not draw in fine design lines and details – these are best omitted or painted on freehand after the stencil has dried.

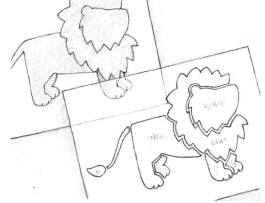

2 Planning colours Study the motif and decide how many colours are required. If necessary simplify the design by reducing the number of colours. Make a second tracing from the first, drawing in simple, strong shapes that are easy to cut out. Colour in the shapes to check the effect.

3 Separating the colours Make a final tracing, this time leaving gaps (bridges) between the large areas of colour. Mark on the design where each colour falls.

4 Sizing the motif Decide whether you need to enlarge or reduce your finished drawing on a photocopier to suit the scale of the item you are stencilling.

TIP

LAYERING COLOUR

To avoid having to bother with detailed registration and cutting lots of awkward bridges, it is possible to stencil smaller areas of a different colour on top of the main colour without leaving any gaps between the two. Plan the colours carefully, so that you paint dark colours on top of pale ones. The look of the second colour is sometimes altered by the first – so check the effect on scrap paper. Mark the overlay areas on the final tracing of your motif.

◁ You don't have to be completely faithful to the design you are adapting. In fact, the best results are often gained by modifying and rearranging the motifs to suit the item being stencilled. On this cupboard door, two giraffes stencilled in mirror image create a balanced design, framed with a trio of leaves in each corner – a feature adapted from a leafy section of the fabric print.

▲ *The whole tiger on this lampshade is stencilled in yellow first, then the red stripes are stencilled directly over the yellow image. Fine details, like his smiling face, are best painted in by hand once the stencil has dried.*

CUTTING THE STENCIL

Whether using a single or multi-sheet stencil, you need to cut registration marks in the edges. These let you space and position the stencil accurately on the item you're stencilling – when repeating the motif in a frieze for example. They're also a useful extra aid when lining up the design on multi-sheet stencils; cut them in identical positions on each sheet.

1 Cutting the stencil sheets
Attach the final tracing to a cutting mat with masking tape. Lay a piece of acetate over the motif and draw a frame round the design, leaving a 2.5cm (1in) margin for strength. Trim the acetate along the frame line. Cut an equal-sized piece for each different colour, if desired.

2 Making the registration marks
For a multi-sheet stencil, stack the sheets, lining up the edges. Cut a V-shaped nick centrally in the two side edges of the stencil sheet(s).

3 Tracing off Tape an acetate sheet over the tracing, shiny side down. On a *multi-sheet stencil*, use the marker pen to trace all areas to be stencilled in one colour with a solid line, and all other areas with a dotted line. On a *single sheet stencil*, trace around all the areas with a solid line.

▶ *The stylized balloon frieze is a cheerful addition to the room. You could either stencil it directly on the wall, or work on a strip of paper and mount it on to the wall in the same way as a wallpaper border. The balloon motif is a good example of bridges at work – without introducing them between the panels of the balloon, the centre panel would fall away from the stencil.*

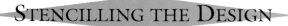

4 Cutting out Remove the acetate from the tracing and tape it shiny side down to the cutting mat. Using a craft knife, cut around the solid outlines and border lines. To ensure a smooth edge, draw the knife towards you and apply even pressure for the entire length of a line. To cut around corners, turn the mat with stencil attached, rather than turning the knife – this will give a smoother, more accurate finish.

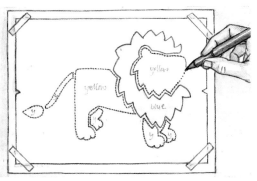

STENCILLING THE DESIGN

Use the appropriate paint or ink for the item you are stencilling. For fabrics, especially items that may need laundering, it is best to use special fabric paints. On walls and accessories, like a paper lampshade, artists' acrylics, pots of stencil paint or even emulsion/latex are suitable.

5 Cutting subsequent stencil sheets (for *multi-sheet stencils*) Retrace the complete motif and border lines on to a second sheet of acetate as in step 3, but this time trace round the areas in a second colour with a solid line and the rest of the design with dotted ones. Cut along the solid lines as in step 4. Repeat this step to cut out a separate stencil for each colour in the motif. Check that you have cut out all the right sections on each colour stencil. Recut if necessary.

SPRAY PAINT STENCILLING

The fine speckled mist of spray paints provides a unique way to colour stencils. With a little practice you can learn how to blend colours and build up a sense of depth in a stencil design.

Decorative, enamel and car spray paints are ideal for stencilling because they are very quick drying. After only a moment or two, you can spray a second coat over the first to strengthen the shade or add a new colour. Unlike other stencil techniques which require you to work the whole design in one colour before moving on to the next shade, spray painting lets you apply all the colours before moving the stencil to the next position. The fine mist which gives such a delicate, hazy effect is also less likely to seep underneath the stencil and form smudges.

For all types of stencilling it's a good idea to test the techniques and colours on scrap material before you embark on the real thing. In the case of spray stencilling this is absolutely vital. Practice enables you to get the feel of the spray canister, how much pressure you need to apply to the nozzle and at what angle and distance you should hold the can from the surface for the best effect.

Try to limit yourself to using only three or four colours, otherwise the stencil looks overworked. By experimenting you will soon discover that you can create a broad spectrum of colours simply by spraying one paint over another so they intermingle. Keep all your test pieces and note the colours you use, so you have an original palette from which you can choose the most flattering way to colour your stencil.

On walls and floors spray paints make light work of an adventurous stencilling project. Green and blue paint are all that you need to colour in this striking collection of oceanic motifs.

HOW TO SPRAY STENCIL

The most important part of spray stencilling is applying the paint so it lightly dusts the surface rather than forming a thick coat. To do this you have to hold the canister well back from the surface and press the nozzle firmly to deliver a short burst of paint. To obtain a more intense colour, spray several thin films of paint over each other. By combining faint and dark areas in this way, you can create a three-dimensional effect in the design. Don't worry if the spray splatters a bit – as long as there are no huge blobs, a few irregular spots look attractive.

A great deal of the charm of spray stencilling lies in the subtle blending of colours and a soft, hazy look, so it doesn't matter if the paint mist strays slightly to other sections of the stencil. If, however, you do want to control the paint direction, you can either mask out areas with tape or use a spray guard, fashioned from a piece of cardboard, to deflect the paint.

Using spray paints is undeniably a messy business, so cover the walls, ground and any items in the work area, indoors or out, with dust sheets, newspaper or plastic sheeting taped or Blu-Tacked in place. Then stick pieces of card all round the stencil to mask the immediate area. To protect yourself, wear old clothing, a face mask and lightweight plastic gloves. Use the paints outside or in a well ventilated area.

Decorative, enamel and car spray paints are suitable for stencilling most surfaces, including fabrics. However, you should avoid using water-based decorative spray paints on fabric items that you might need to wash. Always hand wash or dry clean spray-stencilled fabric.

1 Preparing to stencil
Clean the surface you are stencilling so it is dirt and grease free. Allow it to dry. Protect the surrounding area with dust sheets. Practise using the spray paint and stencils on scrap material or lining paper.

2 Laying out fabric (optional)
If you are working on fabric, iron it perfectly flat and use masking tape to hold it in place over a flat work surface. Slip a piece of cardboard behind the fabric to absorb any paint that seeps through it.

3 Positioning the stencil
Apply a thin coat of spray adhesive to the back of the stencil, carefully position it on the item being stencilled and press it in place. Secure the edges of the stencil with strips of masking tape.

4 Masking out the stencil
Use some masking tape to stick pieces of scrap cardboard all around the sides of the stencil. Carefully cover with masking tape any sections of the stencil that you do not want to spray with paint.

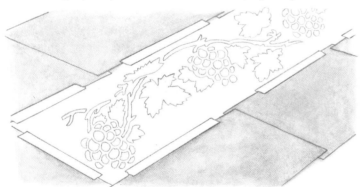

▶ *A mist of green, blue and violet spray paints combine in muted fresco tones on this calico blind. If you plan to spray stencil on a fabric item that will require occasional cleaning, use car or enamel paints and be sure to dry clean or handwash only.*

5 Spraying
Always follow the manufacturer's instructions and practise using each spray paint can before colouring the stencil. Hold the can at a slight angle, about 25cm (10in) from the surface. Press the nozzle to deliver a short, light burst of paint in the desired area of the stencil. Move the can slightly as you spray so the paint does not build up in one area. The colour is touch-dry in a few seconds so you can spray another colour on top.

TIP

SAFETY
The fumes from spray paints are fairly unpleasant and they can be toxic, so you should always be sure to work outside or in a well ventilated room, wearing a face mask. Never use spray paints if you are pregnant.

7 Spraying small details If you need to restrict a colour to a very small area, first cut a hole in a piece of scrap cardboard so that it just reveals the detail to be sprayed, then position the cardboard over the detail. Hold the can about 15cm (6in) away from the stencil and spray lightly through the hole.

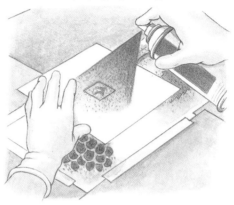

8 Completing the design Remove the masking tape and lift off the stencil. If required, reposition the stencil to continue the design. If you want to reverse the stencil, and once you finish using it, dust the back with talcum powder to deaden the adhesive. On hard surfaces, such as plaster and wood, apply two or three coats of clear polyurethane varnish to protect and seal the finish.

▽ *A row of topiary shrubs is the perfect stencil detail for this handsome planter.*

6 Using spray guards Use pieces of scrap cardboard to direct the spray and prevent colours mixing in certain areas of the stencil. Hold the guard in your free hand so that it masks the desired area of the stencil. For a mottled effect, tear the edges of the guard so that the paint mist spreads slightly around it.

STENCILLED MATTING

Items such as door mats and natural floor matting don't normally spring to mind when it comes to choosing something to stencil on. Their rough texture means the paint is likely to become patchy and clogged, and probably ooze under the edges of the stencil. However with spray paints these difficulties are largely overcome – the fine paint mist settles evenly over almost any surface and dries quickly without clogging.

The results can be unique. You could introduce colour and pattern to a basic woven matting or personalize an inexpensive door mat with a cheerful design or welcoming message.

◨ *The bright colours of this fruity stencil liven up the fibrous weave of the matting and pick out the colour of the edging tape. The basic leaf, fruit and stem shapes of the stencil are simple enough to sketch and cut out yourself from a piece of cardboard.*

◨ *Natural floor matting stencilled in pure white makes for simplicity and sophistication within a subdued colour scheme. Choosing a single colour to work in also means that each stencil you work is a one-step process.*

▶ *The spreading branches of an orange tree on this doormat make a cheerful welcome. To create clean, distinct colours, mask out any sections of stencil you don't want paint to spread to, so the colours can't merge.*

TEXTURED STENCILLING

Add a further dimension to stencilling using textured paint. Make your own 3-D stencils from corrugated card for a raised, sculptured effect, or sponge the paint on a ready-made stencil for a little light relief.

Textured paint is mostly used for covering up cracking plaster or forming relief patterns like combed swirls over a wall or ceiling, but with a little imagination you can take it a step further, using it to create unusual three-dimensional stencils.

The stencil effects you can achieve with textured paint depend on the stencil thickness and how much paint you apply. To make heavily sculptured shapes – akin to roughly cast, plaster mouldings – cut a stencil out of thick card and use it on the wall like a mould for thickly applied textured paint. As intricate designs are tricky to cut out in thick card, and almost impossible to reproduce in textured

paint, it's best to choose a simple, solid shaped motif for this effect. A raised stencil isn't suitable for an area where it's likely to get knocked, for example in a narrow hall.

Less dramatic but equally stylish are the subtler effects formed by using ready-made stencils sponged with textured paint. The light application of textured paint contrasts with a smooth painted background. Almost any design is suitable for sponge stencilling.

For contrasting colour effects with all types of textured stencilling, use the white textured paint on top of a coloured background, or add colour to the textured paint by adding a few drops of a paint tinter.

Leaves moulded from textured paint dance across a golden wall like falling autumn foliage. Taken from a complex border stencil design, the simple leaf shape provides an ideal motif for this type of relief stencilling.

63

RAISED STENCILLING

YOU WILL NEED

❖ EMULSION/LATEX or TEXTURED PAINT (optional)

❖ CORRUGATED CARDBOARD, about 4mm (³⁄₁₆in) thick

❖ CRAFT KNIFE AND CRAFT ADHESIVE

❖ READY-MIXED HEAVY-TEXTURED PAINT

❖ LIDDED CONTAINER (optional)

❖ WATER-BASED PAINT TINTER (optional)

❖ OLD SAUCER

❖ PALETTE KNIFE

❖ LEVEL, RULER and CHALK (optional)

❖ MASKING TAPE

❖ CLOTH

The best type of textured paint for raised stencilling is heavy-textured paint, most commonly used for all-over decorative paint effects on walls and ceilings. It is available in powder form to mix with water, but a more convenient alternative for stencilling is to use the ready-mixed variety sold in a tub. Both types of textured paint come in white only and are available from do-it-yourself stores.

To colour the textured paint, use a paint tinter available from specialist paint suppliers. Paint tinters are very concentrated colours, sometimes sold in a syringe, which you add in drops to the white paint. Mix enough coloured paint for the entire project to ensure a colour match throughout. Store it in a container with a lid, taking small amounts as you need them so that the paint doesn't dry out.

To build up the paint on the wall, use a fairly thick stencil cut from a piece of flat or corrugated cardboard or plastic. Cardboard is more commonly available and is a lot easier to cut out, but plastic has the advantage that you can scrub it clean. Packaging provides a good source of corrugated cardboard and plastic. Experiment on a piece of scrap using stencils cut from different thicknesses. The stencils shown here are cut from 4mm (³⁄₁₆in) corrugated cardboard. Stencils more than 6mm (¼in) thick are difficult to work with because the paint is so thick and heavy.

1 Preparing the walls Prepare the walls as usual, making sure they are sound, clean and dry. If necessary, apply a coat of emulsion or fine textured paint, with a colourwash finish if desired. Allow to dry.

2 Making the stencil Draw your own motif or use a photocopier to enlarge a ready-made stencil, or one of the motifs provided, to the desired size. Stick the motif on to a piece of card then use a craft knife to cut out the stencil.

3 Preparing to stencil If necessary, use a spirit level, ruler and chalk to mark the stencil positions on the wall, using a random or regular pattern as desired. Secure the stencil in position with strips of masking tape.

4 Tinting the paint (optional) Transfer some of the textured paint to a lidded container and gradually mix in a few drops of paint tinter until you achieve the desired shade.

▷ *Simple solid shapes like the abstract leaf motifs shown here and on the previous page are the best choice for raised stencilling. A piece of decorative table linen provides the inspiration for these naive-style textured stencils.*

5 Applying the paint Transfer some of the textured paint – sufficient for one or two stencils – on to an old saucer. Holding the stencil with one hand, take a scoop of textured paint on to the palette knife and apply it into the hollow of the stencil. Spread out the paint to fill the stencil, forcing it gently towards the edges to remove any air bubbles and carefully levelling it flush with the surface.

6 Removing the stencil Still holding the stencil in position, carefully peel off the masking tape. Gently pull away the stencil from the wall, taking care not to disturb the raised motif as you do so. Use the cleaned palette knife to scrape away any paint smears and neaten the edges of the stencilled shape.

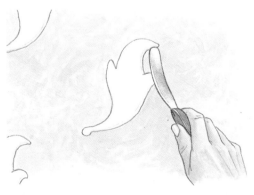

7 Finishing off Scrape off and discard any paint on the stencil, taking care to clear the inside edges and the back. Wipe the back of the stencil with a moist cloth. Continue applying the stencil across the wall. Allow to dry overnight and apply a further paint effect on top if desired.

LIGHT RELIEF STENCILLING

YOU WILL NEED

- ❖ EMULSION/LATEX or FINE TEXTURED PAINT (optional)
- ❖ LEVEL, RULER and CHALK (optional)
- ❖ STENCIL
- ❖ LOW-TACK SPRAY ADHESIVE OR MASKING TAPE (optional)
- ❖ READY-MIXED HEAVY-TEXTURED PAINT
- ❖ LIDDED CONTAINER (optional)
- ❖ WATER-BASED PAINT TINTER (optional)
- ❖ OLD SAUCER
- ❖ SPONGE

Applying heavy-textured paint with a sponge to a ready-made stencil creates a subtle relief effect. Any stencil design is suitable, from the simple to the intricate.

The border design shown here is worked in a single colour, but you could use tinted textured paint or a coloured emulsion paint on top of the textured paint once it's dry. It may help to mask off different colour areas as you work.

For a slightly thicker relief effect, build up layers of paint, one on top of the other in the same or complementary colours. Experiment with the technique on a piece of scrap card before embarking on the wall itself.

1 Securing the stencil Prepare the wall as usual and apply a base coat if desired. Mark the stencil positions if necessary, using a level, ruler and chalk. Secure the stencil in position on the wall using low-tack spray adhesive or masking tape.

2 Preparing to stencil Use a water-based paint tinter to colour batches of textured paint, if desired, and store each colour in a separate lidded container. Transfer small amounts of the paint on to an old saucer as you are working so the bulk of the paint doesn't dry out.

3 Painting the stencil Press a small piece of sponge into the paint and apply to the stencil with a dabbing action. Without smudging the paint, remove the stencil, then reposition it to paint any remaining stencils.

4 Adding another coat (optional) Check the first coat of paint is dry then reposition the stencil over the previously painted motif, matching the stencil outline exactly. Apply a second coat of the same or a different colour of textured paint over the first. Remove the stencil and repeat for the remaining stencils. Allow to dry.

Waves of textured paint, coloured with a few drops of smoky blue paint tinter, roll across a white painted background to form a well defined border. For a more distinct relief effect, sponge more than one coat of paint on to each stencil.

DECORATING FLOORBOARDS

Of all flooring options, wooden floorboards offer the greatest scope for decoration and inventiveness, so why not take to your boards with brushes and paints or stains?

Sanded wooden floorboards invite all manner of decorative finishes from painting and staining to stencilling and stamping – treatments that can be purely for visual interest and ones that also make the surface more hardwearing. On the practical side, the cost of decorating floorboards is considerably less than that of covering them with carpet, vinyl or tiles, so you can afford to go for more exciting design and colour schemes that can be updated with comparative ease the next time you are decorating.

Overall designs that mimic the look of tiled flooring are one of the most popular and straightforward ways to decorate bare boards. You can use tape to mask off a design on a bare or coloured floor, then paint or stain the exposed areas as you prefer. Stencil and stamp designs can be used to create similar all-over patterns or to form a border or centrepiece for the room.

The scope of the floor design is almost unlimited, but it is important to take stock of the condition of the boards before making any decisions. No matter how hard you try to disguise the fact, if they are in a very bad state, it might be more realistic to admit defeat and lay a floorcovering.

For sheer panache, floorboards painted harlequin-style create a look that rivals any type of floorcovering. Careful design planning and accurate measuring and marking ensure that the corners of each square line up with the edge of a floorboard.

67

PLANNING AND PREPARATION

Before you start decorating the floorboards it's crucial to plan and map out the design accurately. Think carefully about the room and how you use it before choosing the colours and pattern. Bear in mind that large patterns and dark colours make a room seem smaller, while more detailed patterns and light colours amplify a feeling of space. If the room is in constant use, keep your design simple and use quick-drying materials.

PAINTS

Almost any type of home-decorating paint is suitable for floorboards – even relatively light-duty emulsion – because it is the layers of varnish applied on top of the paint that provide protection from everyday wear and tear. The varnish also gives the floor its finish, so it's not really worth opting for an expensive gloss paint when a gloss varnish gives the same effect.

Eggshell (flat satin) and emulsion (latex) paints are the best choice for most projects and come in a wide range of colours. Use the appropriate wood primer and undercoat before painting the pattern on top. To conceal a large number of knots and blemishes it's best to use paint rather than stain which would only serve to highlight the defects.

STAINS

Staining floorboards is a good way to add colour without sacrificing the character of the grain and knots. This can be done using wood tones to enhance the natural shade or imitate a more expensive timber. Or you can transform the appearance of the wood with a whole spectrum of rainbow colours.

Stains for wood fall into two main categories: coloured varnishes and lacquers, which impart both colour and protection to the wood; and dyes, available in a wider range of colours, that colour the wood but require a wax polish, oil or clear varnish finish on top.

Whatever type of stain you choose, it's important to do a colour test on an inconspicuous area of the floor. The result depends on the wood grain, its original colour and how much stain is absorbed. Further coats of stain will deepen the colour, so let the first coat be absorbed and test a smaller area with a second coat. You can mix stain colours of the same type to achieve the shade you prefer.

Unlike paint or coloured varnish, which can be sanded off, a wood dye permeates the wood so the effect is permanent.

PREPARING THE FLOOR

No matter how you intend to decorate the floorboards it's vital to prepare them first. If you have just uncovered the floorboards and are uncertain whether they are adequately prepared, test a small hidden area with the paint or varnish you are using. Once the patch has dried, rub the edge with a coin; if any paint or varnish flakes off you need to sand off the existing varnish or wax.

◀ *Sealed beneath several protective coats of clear varnish, the delicate tones of these coloured wood dyes will be preserved for many years.*

Measure the dimensions of the room and draw a scaled-down plan on a piece of squared paper, then map your design ideas on to the scale plan.

Centring With an all-over design the most pleasing results usually come by centring the pattern.

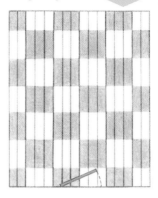

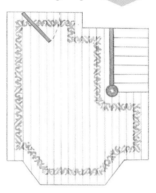

Borders A border design works well to define the outer edges of a room, particularly if the room is an interesting shape.

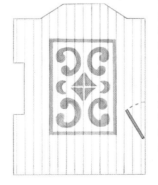

Centrepiece Rather than painting the entire floor space, you could limit the design to a centrepiece or create a clever trompe l'oeil effect – like a fireside rug, for example.

Squaring off In a room with awkward corners and alcoves, or where the walls aren't square, rather than fragment the pattern you can square off the room by working out the largest rectangle that fits into the space, then leave a plain border around the perimeter of the room.

L-shaped or T-shaped rooms Depending on the shape and proportions of the room, you can either treat it as a unified space or work the design in visually linked sections. Centre the design in the main section of the room and then carry the pattern into the remaining sections so the design is continuous. Alternatively, divide the space into rectangles or squares and work each section separately using an all-over, border or centrepiece design.

◥ *Almost any type of decorating paint is suitable for painting floorboards, so you can plan a coordinated colour scheme to flow uninterrupted between the walls, woodwork and floor.*

PAINTING A CHEQUERBOARD

Most all-over painted floor patterns – chequered, lattice, diamond or triangular – are based on a grid of lines drawn at 45° or 90° to the boards. This type of pattern works best in a rectangular room, or one that has been squared off.

Use your room scale plan to experiment with different spacing, angles and colour combinations, centring the design, squaring off the room and creating a border as necessary. Try to adjust the size of the squares or other pattern repeat so there are complete runs, particularly along the most dominant walls of the room. If you want a pattern to align with the edges of the floorboards, let the width of a floorboard determine the scale of the design, so the lines are either two, three or four board-widths apart; you may also need to shift the centrepoint slightly so it falls along the edge of the nearest board. Where the walls are not square it is generally better to align a pattern with the floorboards than with the walls.

With a two-colour chequered design that has an all-over base colour, it is usual to apply the lighter colour as the base coat, otherwise the darker colour may show through the top coat.

▲ *This two-colour chequer design comprises a buttermilk background – painted over the entire floor – and a darker slate wash applied on top to squares.*

1 Preparing to paint Clear the room completely. Prepare and sand the boards to a clean, smooth finish. Draw a scale plan of your design.

2 Applying a base coat (optional) For an all-over painted base coat, apply a coat of primer and undercoat followed by two coats of the base colour. Alternatively apply a stain or coat of varnish. Allow each coat to dry thoroughly and sand lightly between coats, removing any dust with a vacuum cleaner.

3 Finding the design centrepoint Find the midpoint of each wall or of each side of the squared off area. Pin two lengths of string across the floor between the midpoints, so they divide the area into quarters. If necessary, adjust the strings slightly to align with the floorboards or for a whole number of squares or pattern repeats on either side; or centre one line on a chimney breast.

4 Marking the centrepoint Use a set square to check that the strings cross at right angles, then rub them with chalk and snap them to leave chalk lines. With a pencil, mark clearly the centrepoint where the lines cross.

5 Transferring the design Following your scale plan and working from the centrepoint outwards, use a ruler and pencil to mark the position of the squares in the chequer pattern – you may find it helps to use a card, wood or tile template to measure and mark. Check each right angle because any discrepancies will become exaggerated as the pattern builds up.

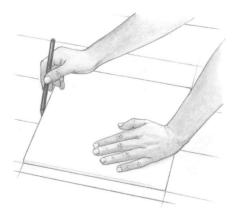

7 Scoring the edges (optional) To prevent stains bleeding from one area to another, use a sharp craft knife and metal straightedge to score lightly along the borders of the pattern.

8 Painting the floor Starting at the corner furthest from the door, use a paint brush to apply paint or varnish, or a lint-free cloth to apply stain, to the masked off areas. Apply the paint or stain following the wood grain.

9 Completing the painting Allow the paint or stain to dry thoroughly and apply further coats if necessary. Carefully peel off the masking tape. If necessary mask off further squares and paint or stain them as before.

10 Varnishing the floor Once the floor is completely dry apply two or more coats of clear floor varnish, allowing each coat to dry and sanding lightly between coats.

▼ *Floorboards decorated with a patchwork of bare and painted squares and topped with a satin finish varnish look perfect in this luxurious room and are created with the minimum of cost.*

6 Masking off the squares Following the guide lines marked on the floor, use low-tack masking tape to mask off alternate dark squares, or other squares as appropriate to your design. Make sure that the masking tape meets neatly at the corners and is firmly pressed down so that paint can't spread underneath it.

STENCILS AND STAMPS

Stencils and stamps can be used imaginatively to create all-over and border designs or to add a focal point such as an imitation rug on bare or coloured floorboards. The techniques employed combine those for preparing the boards and planning a floor design with those used in ordinary stencilling or stamping.

Both paints and stains are suitable for floor stencilling; however, for a stamped floor design only paints can be used. For more detailed patterns with several repeats it is easiest to work with quick-drying paints, such as emulsion or artists' acrylic thinned with water, so you don't have to wait long for a painted section to dry before continuing with the next area. These types of paint also come in a good range of colours. Spray paints are an alternative for stencilling. If you are stencilling with wood dyes, use a lint-free cloth to apply the minimum of stain so it goes on evenly and does not leak under the stencil.

With an all-over pattern you can position individual motifs randomly over the floor or measure and mark out a grid that ensures each motif is evenly spaced. Once the design is complete and fully dry, finish off with two or more protective coats of clear varnish.

▲ A stamp is a quick way to create a repeating pattern over a floor. Depending on the design, either mark out a grid to make sure you position each stamp in exactly the right place or trust in the charm of a less precise effect worked by eye.

◀ A stencil pattern designed to look like an oriental rug adds a cosy touch to a bathroom where the real thing would be impractical. In an area of the home such as the bathroom, it's important to use quick-drying paints or stains and varnish so the area won't be out of action for long.

MOSAIC BLOCK PRINTING

*Have fun making your own simple printing blocks
from potatoes or offcuts of wood to create multi-coloured mosaic effect
patterns on plain furniture, rugs and fabric.*

P rinted with handmade wood or potato block prints, mosaic patterns are a classic decoration for all sorts of plain surfaces. Built up of small square, rectangular or triangular motifs, the mosaic designs can be as simple or as complicated as you like, ranging from a basic chequer-board pattern to an ornate pictorial design.

To print the designs you need to make a separate print block for each colour, cutting the appropriate shape out of potato or wood. Straight lines are easier to cut than a continuous curve. Then you simply coat the block motifs with paint and press them against the surface to transfer the impression. Don't worry if the print effect is slightly mottled or the mosaic pattern isn't per-fectly regular – real mosaic is never exactly uniform and small variations only reinforce the charm of the handprinted look.

Small items of furniture and simple accessories with square or rectangular flat surfaces, such as drawer fronts, book covers and place mats, are a good starting point for printing mosaics. Once you've mastered a flat surface, you might consider decorating a curved item, such as a lamp base or shade. In this case you need to roll the print block around the curved surface.

Using the appropriate craft paints, you can print on all sorts of surfaces – adding decoration to plain chinaware, ceramic tiles, glass, fabric accessories and furnishings, even walls or concrete and wooden floors.

This floor rug, made from thick felt edged with carpet tape, provides the base for a two-tone potato print mosaic design. To create your own mosaic designs, use a piece of squared paper to map out the individual mosaic motifs then enlarge the mosaic grid pattern and transfer it on to the surface.

The mosaic-effect pattern on this cupboard is printed using square, wooden print blocks, made from offcuts of timber faced on one side with a felt pad to hold the paint. You can make the print blocks whatever size you want, depending on the scale of the mosaic design, the item you are decorating and the size of the timber available. In this case the blocks are 32mm (1¼in) square.

Timber merchants and do-it-yourself stores with a timber cutting service are likely to have inexpensive timber offcuts. Because the print blocks spoil if you wash them repeatedly, it's best to make one block for each paint colour. This also means you can apply the different coloured paints in the same painting session and see the multi-coloured pattern building up quickly.

PAINTS

The motifs are printed on top of a lighter coloured emulsion base coat. A narrow gap – representing grouting – is left between each motif. When marking the guidelines, allow for this gap.

To print the mosaic design, use paint with a creamy consistency, such as artists' acrylic or emulsion paints. You can use these for printing on furniture, accessories, walls and ceilings.

CIRCULAR SURFACE

Although it is much easier to work a mosaic design on a square or rectangular surface, the effect also looks very effective on a circular surface, such as a round table top. With a circle it's usual to work the mosaic from the centre outwards. Measure and mark the centre point of the surface and print the mosaic motifs spiralling outwards from it to the edge.

YOU WILL NEED

❖ CUPBOARD or other piece of furniture
❖ ABRASIVE PAPER
❖ PRIMER (optional)
❖ EMULSION/LATEX PAINT BASE COAT
❖ PAINT BRUSH
❖ TIMBER OFFCUT, 32mm (1¼in) square
❖ TAPE MEASURE
❖ TRY/L SQUARE
❖ TENON SAW
❖ FELT
❖ SCISSORS
❖ ALL-PURPOSE, WATERPROOF ADHESIVE
❖ CHALK and RULER
❖ ACRYLIC or EMULSION/LATEX PAINTS in selection of colours
❖ GOLD FOIL (optional)
❖ PVA ADHESIVE (optional)
❖ CLEAR MATT ACRYLIC SPRAY

TIP

HIDING MISTAKES

If you make any printing mistakes, allow the paint to dry then sand off carefully with fine grade abrasive paper or wire wool and print again. Alternatively, allow to dry, paint over the mistake with the base colour, allow to dry and start again. If the print effect is not even, spread a little paint over the print block motif and apply the print again.

1 Preparing the item Make sure the surface being decorated is sound and clean. Remove any loose paint and sand the surface smooth. Apply a coat of primer to bare wood or metal and allow to dry. Apply one or two coats of base coat, sanding between coats.

2 Making the print blocks Measure and mark a length of timber about 4cm (1½in) long. Use a try square to carry the marks around the sides of the wood and cut to length with a tenon saw. Sand off any rough edges. Cut a square of felt to match the sawn face of the wood and stick in place with all-purpose, waterproof adhesive. Make blocks for each colour in the same way.

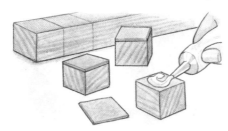

3 Marking the mosaic grid Decide on the spacing between each mosaic motif – in this case about 3mm (⅛in). Centring the first column of squares midway across each surface being decorated, use a ruler and chalk to mark a grid pattern where each square equals the mosaic motif size plus the spacing. If necessary, adjust the spacing slightly at the edges to fit in a whole number of squares, or allow the squares to overlap the edges.

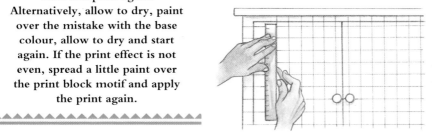

4 Priming the print blocks Pour a small amount of each paint colour on to separate dishes. Using a different print block for each colour, press the felt pad of the print block lightly into the paint. Practise printing on scrap paper until the print is uniform.

5 Printing the mosaic Start printing on the furniture surface, using the chalk grid as a guide for positioning the motifs. Apply different colours to create a random or regular mosaic pattern, as preferred. If desired, leave a few grid squares blank and decorate these following step 6.

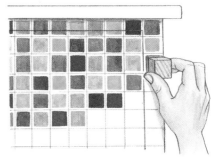

6 Adding gold foil squares (optional) Cut out squares of gold foil from sweet or candy wrappers the same size as the mosaic motifs. Stick the foil squares on to the blank squares of the grid, applying a little PVA adhesive to the surface being decorated.

7 Finishing off Allow to dry thoroughly. Rub off the chalk guidelines. Apply two coats of clear matt acrylic spray, allowing to dry completely between coats.

▶ *This wooden cupboard is elevated from being very plain to eye-catching designer status by printing it with a multi-coloured mosaic design, interspersed with candy-wrapper gold squares.*

PRINTING ON FABRIC

The tablecloth and napkin shown here are decorated with a potato print mosaic, using water-based liquid fabric paints. These are available from art and craft suppliers and by mail order.

For best results, print on medium- to heavyweight cotton or linen with a smooth surface. First wash the fabric in a mild detergent, without fabric softener, then press it. Mark out the mosaic pattern using dressmakers' chalk or, for fine lines, an air erasable pen, available from fabric/sewing shops – the lines fade after a day or two.

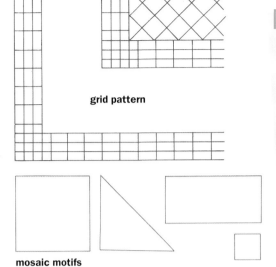

grid pattern

mosaic motifs

1 Preparing the fabric Wash and press the tablecloth and napkins. Cover the work surface with a sheet of polythene. Lay the tablecloth or a napkin flat on the work surface and secure the edges with masking tape.

2 Marking the grid pattern Enlarge the grid pattern provided or create your own design. Using a ruler and air erasable pen or dressmakers' chalk, transfer the grid pattern on to the fabric.

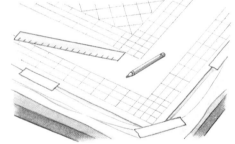

3 Cutting potato print blocks Enlarge the mosaic motifs to the desired size. Cut a potato in half; using a ruler and felt tip pen, draw the outline of one mosaic motif on to the cut face. With a kitchen knife, cut away the potato outside the outline, leaving the motif as a raised area. Make print blocks for the other motifs in the same way.

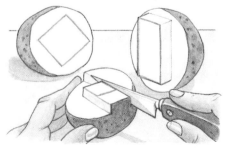

4 Printing the pattern Use an artists' brush to apply fabric paint to the potato motif. Practise on scrap fabric until you achieve a uniform print effect. With one colour at a time, print the motifs on the fabric, using the grid lines as a guide. Allow to dry, then remove the cloth from the table. Fix the paint following the manufacturer's instructions.

▶ *Jazz up a white tablecloth and napkins with a colourful mosaic centrepiece and border using fabric paints and potato print blocks.*

FURNITURE FACELIFTS

Revamping furniture that's past its prime is child's play when you use splashes of brightly coloured paint and simple patterns – and all in little time and at pocket money prices.

There is a vast range of elaborate decorative and faux paint effects that you can use to revamp items of furniture that are somewhat less than distinguished, but sometimes the very simplest solutions are the best. Unfussy, hand-painted designs worked in solid, vibrant colours fit well in contemporary, colour conscious interiors, and with a slightly naive approach, are not out of place in an imaginative, traditional home.

The charm of this hand-painted furniture lies largely in the casual way it is painted. This can range from controlled geometric repetition, such as diamonds and stripes, to freehand patterns and motifs formed and even devised as the paint hits the surface. If the paint overlaps or smudges, you can simply leave it that way, wipe it off or allow it to dry and repaint on top, so there is no need to worry about making mistakes – just have fun experimenting.

Wooden furniture that is past its best and doesn't warrant antique status, as well as inexpensive factory-made and flat-pack furniture, can be quickly rejuvenated with a splash or two of bright paint. Smaller pieces, such as trays, planters or kitchen cupboard doors, are also good candidates. A paint cover-up using the same colours and pattern is also a good way to coordinate a batch of completely mismatched items.

This colourful painted chest of drawers echoes the pattern of stripy blind fabric and the colours of various table and decorative accessories. The lively pattern of the paintwork also reflects the framed artwork above.

COLOURS GALORE

Quick-drying paints such as emulsion (latex) or, for smaller projects, artists' acrylic are ideal for a quick facelift. For a multi-coloured paint palette, buy a selection of tester pots of emulsion paint. These are relatively inexpensive, available in every colour and mean less wastage if you want to use several colours. Use solvent-based gloss or eggshell (satin) paints to decorate a plastic laminate surface, such as melamine kitchen cabinets.

PREPARATION

Preparation is important for all types of paintwork but don't let endless hours of stripping and fine sanding put you off a project. Give each piece the preparation time it merits without destroying your enthusiasm before you get round to raising a paint brush. The existing finish – whether bare wood, laminate, varnish or paint – determines the type of preparation required.

In all cases make sure the furniture or accessory you're working on is sound, and use plastic wood filler to fill any cracks and holes. Stripping a painted or varnished piece back to bare wood is not usually necessary – simply wash the surface with sugar soap (an alkaline cleansing preparation for paint) and sand it smooth. But if the existing paint or varnish is very cracked, wrinkled or flaking, remove it using a chemical stripper.

Bare wood and board as well as plastic laminates need priming before painting. Seal any knots in wood with knotting then apply a coat of wood primer to bare wood or board. Key plastic laminated surfaces with abrasive paper, wipe over with white/mineral spirit then prime with gloss paint diluted with 10% white spirit.

▶ *An assortment of kitchen chairs collected from junk shops and flea markets sits together happily once visually linked in shades of green and blue paint.*

PAINTING A TRAY

A regular squared-off patchwork of hand-painted hearts makes a simple and striking decoration for an accessory with a flat surface, such as a wooden tray. A relatively small item is a good choice for a first painting project, since the preparation is minimal and the results are quite quickly achieved, but it is still a good opportunity for experimenting with different colour and pattern effects.

Applying the base coats Prepare the tray surface as described above. Use a decorators' paint brush to apply a coloured base coat of emulsion or artists' acrylic paint. Allow to dry, then lightly rub the surface with fine grade abrasive paper. Apply a second coat of paint and sand as before.

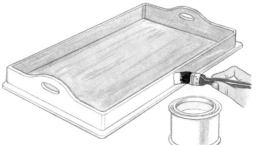

Sketching the design outlines (optional) Using a soft pencil, lightly sketch on the main pattern or motif outlines – in this case the chequered patterns and heart motifs. For a freehand effect, avoid any exact measuring and try not to use any templates or stencils.

Painting the tray Using a clean decorators' or artists' paint brush for each colour, apply the paint to the tray, colouring in the main areas of pattern so the base colour does not show through. Allow to dry. If you are not happy with any of the paint colours or want to build up stronger colours, apply further coats of paint on top as desired.

YOU WILL NEED

- ❖ WOODEN TRAY
- ❖ DECORATORS' AND ARTISTS' PAINT BRUSHES
- ❖ EMULSION/LATEX or ARTISTS' ACRYLIC PAINTS
- ❖ FINE GRADE ABRASIVE PAPER
- ❖ SOFT PENCIL (optional)
- ❖ CLEAR MATT OR SATIN POLYURETHANE VARNISH

4 **Adding the details** Using a clean artists' paint brush for each colour, paint the details such as the striped, spotted and chequered patterns on the hearts. Highlight the inside of the tray handles with a contrast paint colour if you wish. Allow to dry and add further pattern details on top if desired.

▲ *Using uncomplicated patterns and paintbox colours, painting becomes child's play – there are no rules, mistakes don't matter and great results don't take forever.*

5 **Finishing off** For a scuff- and water-resistant finish, apply two or three coats of clear polyurethane varnish. Allow each coat to dry before applying the next.

COLOUR AND PATTERN

The beauty of this informal, naive style of painting is that there are no hard and fast rules for creating patterns or the number and variety of colours you can use. But if you want a degree of coordination, try matching the colours to other items in a room – walls, floor rugs, fabric and ceramics, for example. Pick some of the predominant colours in the room or pinpoint accent colours that you want to highlight.

Alternatively, you can start from scratch and use the piece of painted furniture to introduce fresh bursts of colour; then let the paint shades drift elsewhere – to other furniture and accessories, wooden mouldings, walls and floors.

▲ *A little colourful, geometric tomfoolery worked on this inexpensive kitchen table makes a singular piece from a mass produced item.*

▼ *Decorated with abstract, experimental patterns in colours inspired by a woven floor rug, this wooden dresser makes use of the left-over paint pots and testers used to paint doors and mouldings.*

▲ *Fun has got the upper hand in this painted bathroom – where Aztec-style castellations spread across the vanity unit and walls, whimsical squiggles decorate the lower wall and doodles adorn the rocking chair.*

HAND PAINTING DESIGNS

Examples of decorative hand painting stretch from ancient times to the present day, adding delightful individuality to almost any surface, whether a small piece of furniture or a plastered wall or ceiling.

Although the finished results might suggest otherwise, hand painting doesn't necessarily rely on a high level of artistic talent. With the help of patterns traced from favourite images, and transfer outlines to guide your brushstrokes, what looks like freehand painting is in fact a controlled and repeatable process.

Hand painting has been used over the centuries as a method of home decoration and it's sometimes possible to identify the origins of a piece as the work of an individual crafts person, community or country just by looking at the decorative designs. These are often painted with the help of patterns and the designs sometimes borrowed – directly, or with a few changes and

additions – from those of other artists or cultures. With this historical precedent it's quite in keeping to borrow images from elsewhere to create your own hand-painted design.

Taking your cues from the item that you are working on – its material, shape, colour and condition – look for images that complement these features as well as the surrounding decorative scheme. The most convincing results are usually achieved if you limit yourself to a particular theme rather than mixing styles – for example a dainty 18th-century flower and ribbon design would not work with an Aztec motif. Collect as many appropriate images as possible so you have a choice as you combine and arrange them.

This elegant old chest of drawers is hand-painted with interlocking floral, foliage and decorative linear motifs, emphasizing the form of the chest and integrating the handles into the design.

DESIGN PLANNING

Choose a small item, such as a tray or the back rail of a chair, as a first project and paint it with a simple design; you can buy unpainted blanks for this purpose from craft suppliers. Or, if you want to decorate a large area such as the walls, floor or ceiling, restrict your design to a simple border, centrepiece or corner detail.

DESIGN IDEAS

Draw a scaled-down plan of the surface you're decorating on a piece of paper and sketch on your design ideas. To save time and avoid making the overall effect too busy, consider using pattern repeats or adapting designs.

Corner motifs Create a right-angled corner design and turn it to a different angle to fit each corner of the surface.

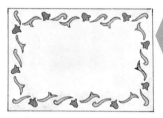

Border repeats Devise a border pattern made up of a series of simple repeating motifs, then join the motifs end to end to form a border.

Extending or reducing a design Create one basic design and adapt it for use on different areas by adding or subtracting elements of the design.

Design details Take a small part of the main design, such as a bud or leaf, and use it elsewhere on the surface being decorated, as a border repeat or other detail.

Mirror image Flip a design top to bottom or side to side for a balanced look. For perfect symmetry, arrange the motifs to make half the design, trace the outlines, then flip the tracing and outline again on the other side.

▲ *The horizontal lines of this chest of drawers are emphasized by three floral and ribbon motifs, each slightly different but using the same components. The blue base colour consists of a mid-blue emulsion (latex) with a coat of white emulsion dragged on top.*

CREATING A DESIGN

The first stage of designing is to collect decorative images to fit your theme. Browse through magazines, fabric and wallpaper books, catalogues for ceramic tiles and tableware, children's illustrations and wrapping paper, looking for motifs with well defined, simple lines, such as flowers, leaves, seashells or butterflies. Choose a few motifs that work well together to use in your design and include various orientations and sizes of the motif, for example different types of ribbon twisting in various ways or full and side views of flowers and buds. If necessary use a photocopier to enlarge or reduce the sizes.

YOU WILL NEED

- ❖ DESIGN IMAGES
- ❖ FINE LINE DRAWING PEN
- ❖ TRACING PAPER
- ❖ SCISSORS
- ❖ RULER and PENCIL
- ❖ WHITE PAPER
- ❖ MASKING TAPE
- ❖ PASTEL PENCIL
- ❖ HARD LEAD PENCIL

1 Tracing the motifs
Prepare the surface to be decorated, applying a paint effect or clear wood sealer as preferred. Simplifying the images to basic outline drawings, use a fine line drawing pen to trace the motifs on to a sheet of tracing paper, leaving a space around each motif for cutting out. Use scissors to cut out the motifs leaving a rough border around each one.

2 Making a pattern
Measure the area being decorated, if necessary dividing a large or awkwardly shaped area into manageable sections. Transfer the measurements on to tracing paper, using a sheet for each section if required. Mark on the pattern the position of any mouldings or fixings and other guidelines, for example the centrepoint or midline for a centred design. Mark similar guidelines on the surface being decorated.

4 Creating a master design Place a sheet of tracing paper over the motifs and secure with masking tape. Using a fine line drawing pen, trace off the motif outlines and any pattern guidelines. Repeat for other sections if necessary.

3 Arranging the motifs
Place the pattern on a sheet of white paper. Arrange the motif cutouts on the pattern, using the guidelines to help you. When you are pleased with the arrangement secure the motifs with small pieces of masking tape, but don't obscure the motif outlines.

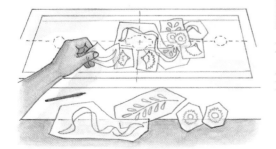

5 Transferring the design Lightly rub over the back of the master design with a pastel pencil. Place the design face up on the surface being decorated, matching the guidelines. Secure in position with masking tape. Trace firmly over the motif outlines with a hard lead pencil to transfer the design. Remove the master design. Repeat for other pattern sections. Rub pastel pencil over the back of the design for each application.

Decorative Brushstrokes

For most hand painting projects you need three good quality artists' brushes: a round brush, size 6 or 7; a flat or one-stroke brush, size 6mm (¼in); and a liner or detail brush, size 2 or 3. Use synthetic water colour brushes if you are using acrylic paint and synthetic sable brushes with oil paint.

For most surfaces the best choice of paint is artists' acrylic paint used on top of a compatible water-based paint or sealer. Otherwise use artists' oil paints on surfaces with a solvent-based finish. Each type of paint can be mixed to create the exact colours you need. Select a few toning colours from your source material or match colours with your existing scheme.

Take time to experiment with the paint colours and brushstrokes on a piece of scrap paper. Use the brush lightly and freely – this comes with confidence – so the brushstrokes create the effect. To help decide which brushstrokes to use, look at the shapes of your motif outlines and compare them with the brushstrokes below.

Lines Use a detail or liner brush or the chiselled edge of a flat brush for fine lines. Load with paint, touch the tip of the brush on the surface and draw it across with an even pressure. For broader lines use a round brush, increasing pressure so the bristles splay out.

Pull stroke Load a flat brush. Holding the broad edge of the brush square to the direction of the stroke, draw the brush across the surface. Lift off the brush at once to form a clean edge. To angle the ends of a pull stroke, or to narrow the stroke, hold the brush at an angle to the direction of the stroke.

Concertina pleats Load a flat brush. Alternating between a *line stroke* made with the chiselled edge, and a *pull stroke* made with the broad edge, draw the brush across the surface in a zigzag movement.

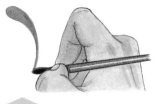

Comma stroke Load a round brush. Touch the brush on the surface and apply pressure to form a rounded start to the stroke. Draw the brush across the surface to form a curve, gradually releasing the pressure so the bristles draw together into a clean point as you lift the brush off the surface.

Ragged comma stroke Load a round brush then dab it on a paper towel to remove most of the paint. Make a comma stroke but, as you release the pressure, drag the tip of the brush over the surface to create a tapering, broken paint effect.

Circle Load a round brush with paint. Holding the brush upright, make a small, circular comma stroke where the tail of the stroke joins up with the head. You can repeat the stroke on top to paint in any gaps.

Tear-drop Form the stroke in the same way as a comma stroke but do not curve it.

Flat brush S-stroke Load the brush with paint. Hold at an angle and draw the chiselled edge of the brush across the surface. Gradually change the direction of the stroke so the broad edge is pulled across the surface to form a curve. Change direction again, shifting back on to the chiselled edge to form an S-shape. Lift off the brush cleanly as the stroke tapers.

Round brush S-stroke Load the brush with paint. Draw the pointed tip of the brush lightly across the surface in a sweeping S-shape, applying slightly more pressure in the middle of the stroke so the bristles widen and then taper.

Tear-drop Form the stroke in the same way as a comma stroke but do not curve it.

Leaf shape Form the stroke as for a round brush S-stroke but do not curve it.

C-stroke Use a flat or round brush and form the stroke in a similar way to the S-stroke but this time changing the direction of the final sweep of the brush so it forms a crescent shape.

Dots Dip the wooden end of the brush in paint and tap it quickly on the surface. The dots will decrease in size as the paint is used up. Use the tip of a cocktail stick for smaller dots and a matchstick for tiny squares.

flat brush

detail brush

round brush

PAINTING

You can mix all the shades of artists' acrylic paint used to decorate this chest of drawers using six colours: ultramarine, spectrum yellow, spectrum red, burnt umber, burnt sienna and white. For green, mix spectrum yellow, ultramarine, white and a dash of burnt umber. For rust, mix burnt umber and white, adding a little spectrum yellow or red to vary the shades. For lilac, mix ultramarine, white and a little spectrum red. For the shaded effects, to lighten colour add a drop of white, and to darken add burnt sienna.

The flower and ribbon design shown here is painted with the following brushstrokes. Paint the ribbons with a flat brush using S- and C-strokes. For leaves use a round brush to form tear-drop and leaf shapes. The facing flowers have a circular centre surrounded with C-stroke petals, paint petal highlights with round brush S-strokes. Paint the flowers and buds in profile with a round brush using comma and tear-drop shapes. Finally, add stem and flower details using a detail or liner brush to paint lines and dots.

If you want to reproduce the designs on the chest of drawers shown here, use a photocopier to enlarge the picture.

A piece of highly decorative printed fabric provides the design inspiration for this hand-painted table. Combining some of the fabric motifs with other design sources means you can create an exclusive design.

YOU WILL NEED

- ARTISTS' ACRYLIC PAINTS
- SAUCERS FOR MIXING PAINT
- ARTISTS' WATER COLOUR BRUSHES: ROUND BRUSH, FLAT BRUSH and DETAIL BRUSH
- SCRAP PAPER
- PAPER TOWEL
- CLOTH
- FINE-GRADE ABRASIVE PAPER (optional)
- HOUSEHOLD PAINT BRUSH, 25mm (1in)
- CLEAR MATT ACRYLIC VARNISH

1 **Preparing to paint** Plan your work sequence: paint the main colour areas first, then fill in the smaller motifs and finally add the fine details. On a saucer, use a brush to mix small amounts of artists' acrylic paint, diluted with a dash of water, to the desired shade. The paint should have a smooth, flowing consistency. Test the colour and consistency on scrap paper.

2 **Painting the design** Select an appropriate shape and size artists' brush. Dip the bristle tips into the paint to load the brush and dab off any excess on a paper towel. With the transfer outlines to guide you, and using the skills noted on the following page, colour in the motifs using the brushstrokes described. Wipe off any mistakes with a damp cloth as you work. Once the main design is coloured, use a detail brush to add the fine details. Allow to dry.

3 **Finishing off** If you want to create a distressed look, lightly rub the surface with fine-grade abrasive paper. Protect the surface with two coats of clear matt acrylic varnish.

PAINTING SKILLS

There are a number of techniques you can employ in hand painting to create more realistic and subtle effects. Combine these skills with the basic brushstrokes to achieve a really professional looking finish.

Follow the motif shape Avoid painting the outline then filling in the middle; this leaves a dark outline which is difficult to disguise. Instead apply the paint in full brushstrokes, allowing the brush to follow the shape of the motif.

Work from dark to light To achieve shade and light, start each brushstroke at the darkest point of the design and finish at the palest point so the colour fades as the paint is lost from the brush. On a flower, for example, you usually need to start the brushstroke at the centre and work out towards the ends of the petals; on a twisting ribbon, start the brushstrokes at the twists so this part looks more shaded.

Colour adjustments If you want a colour to be more intense, don't dilute the paint, and dab the brush on a paper towel to remove excess. Apply the paint then allow to dry and repaint. If the colour is too intense, dab it while still wet with a dry paper towel to lift off some paint.

Distressed effect Allow the paint to dry slightly and then dab it off, to create a distressed look. Once the paint is completely dry you can also rub the surface very lightly with abrasive paper.

Colour tones For a subtle and realistic look combine several shades and tones of one colour. For example, mix up two or three shades of green and paint leaves with different greens; or use a different green to add highlight or shade over another.

Long lines If you are painting long lines, such as leaf stems or tendrils, do not try to paint a continuous line unless you are very practised. Instead make a series of short dashing strokes to give the impression of joining stems.

◀ *Small items and simple designs are a good starting point for hand painting projects. Using pattern repeats and mirror images cuts down on the process of creating the designs.*

PAINTED FIREPLACES

It's easy to give character to a nondescript fireplace, or even create the image of a fireplace surround where none exists, by using textured or patterned paint effects.

Fireplaces form the focal point of a room, and just as well chosen and skilfully applied cosmetics can do wonders, creative paintwork can transform an unmemorable fireplace into an unforgettable one. As well as adding colour, you can change the tone of a fireplace – transforming a formal fireplace, for example, into an informal one – or even create a humorous one in a child's bedroom. For a formal mood, paint classical friezes and column-like pilasters with swag, grapevine or acanthus leaf motifs on a plain fireplace. If a fireplace already has a three-dimensional pattern, you can use it as the basis for your decoration, colouring it in as you would the images in a colouring book.

Patterns on wallpaper, rugs, curtains or upholstery fabrics in the room can be an inspiration, as can paintings or prints hung nearby.

Unless you are experienced, however, do a trial run first, practising your technique on paper to get the pattern and proportion of colours just right. Finally, if your fireplace is a genuine antique, consider carefully the cost and likelihood of successfully restoring it to its original state, should you wish to in the future. Bear in mind that tastes change – Victorian and Art Deco fireplaces, for example, were once despised – and though you may not like the fireplace's style now, you should think twice before destroying its long-term value.

Painted fireplace effects can range from subtle trompe l'oeil to the frankly fake. This simple fireplace is enhanced with classical tracery painted in a slightly darker tone than the background, to mimic the shadows of bas relief.

◀ *A trompe l'oeil triumph*, the illusion of a three-dimensional fireplace is created entirely through paintwork, with a simple shelf forming a substitute mantelpiece. Child-like geometric patterns fill the lintel space, and a flower-filled vase on each side echoes the simple floral paintings in the painted, ochre panel above.

▶ *A disused fireplace* in a children's bedroom is transformed with a painted MDF (medium density fibreboard) panel into a toy theatre, with a two-level stage filling the much reduced proscenium arch opening. Hand-painted fantasy plants and creatures and lively geometric patterns help soften the fireplace's architectural formality.

◀ *Genuine marble fireplaces* can be successfully mimicked – at a fraction of the cost – with paintwork marbling. Here, the fireplace surround and inner frame are treated differently but you could apply the same treatment overall or paint each panel in subtly different shades or patterns.

DECORATIVE LINING

An unfussy style that stands sharply out from the crowd, lining gives a decorative finish and a distinctive edge to plain painted furniture and accessories.

Lining is one of the simplest ways to add distinction to plain wooden furniture and accessories. Use it to give a touch of class to a plain, low-cost table or chest, for example, or a wooden tray. Fine painted lines tracing the contours of the piece add emphasis to individual design elements as well as definition to the overall shape. The position of the lines can serve to alter visually the proportions of the furniture, a line further in from the edge drawing the eye inward to make the item appear more compact.

Lining, which can be applied to most smooth painted surfaces, is usually worked freehand in a contrasting or toning colour to the base paint. The line can be lighter or darker than the base; if you choose a light colour,

you need to make sure that it's opaque enough to show up. Special swordliner paint brushes or lining fitches, both available from art shops, are the best tools for applying an uninterrupted fine line because their long bristles hold a lot of paint. Artists' sable brushes provide a satisfactory alternative.

The idea of freehand painting can be a little daunting, but summon up your courage – confidence is a key factor. Practise on the edge of a scrap piece of board or paper, trying to keep a steady hand. If the results aren't perfect, don't worry: some evidence of hand painting is part of the charm. On the following pages are suggestions to help you prevent imperfections or touch up mistakes, and tricks to achieve a good result.

Hand painted between a creamy base coat and an antique-effect crackle varnish, a watery red line adds stylish definition to the inner and outer contours of this wooden tray.

LINING TECHNIQUES

To achieve an even, uninterrupted flow of the lining paint, the surface you are working on must be very smooth. If you are applying a base paint, rub the surface between coats with fine grade abrasive paper. Or, if the item is already painted but feels slightly rough, apply a coat of clear varnish and, when this is dry, rub very lightly until smooth with fine grade abrasive paper.

A simple precautionary measure that enables you to correct most lining mistakes is to apply a thin coat of clear varnish over the painted base. You can then wipe away any smudges or mistakes with a cotton ball moistened with water or white spirit, depending on the paint you are using.

PAINTS AND BRUSHES

Which paint you use for lining depends on the look you want to achieve. For a faded, watery line use artists' acrylic paint diluted in a little water; for a crisp line dissolve artists' oil paint in a little white spirit. To improve the flow and body of the paint you can add a dash of clear matt water- or oil-based varnish.

Both lining fitches and swordliner brushes have long shaped bristles that allow you to apply a continuous line without needing to recharge the brush. Otherwise, artists' sable brushes are a good substitute – use a 3-12mm (⅛-½in) No 6 brush for broad lines and a 1.5mm (¹⁄₁₆in) No 3 brush for fine lines.

Practise lining along the edge of a scrap piece of board until you get the feel of the brush and paint. Take care to keep the pressure even – this affects the spread of the bristles and therefore the thickness of the line. Practise painting broad and fine lines, using the tip of the brush for fine lines. It can also be helpful, particularly when drawing curves, to mark the lining position with very light touches of paint before starting the lining process.

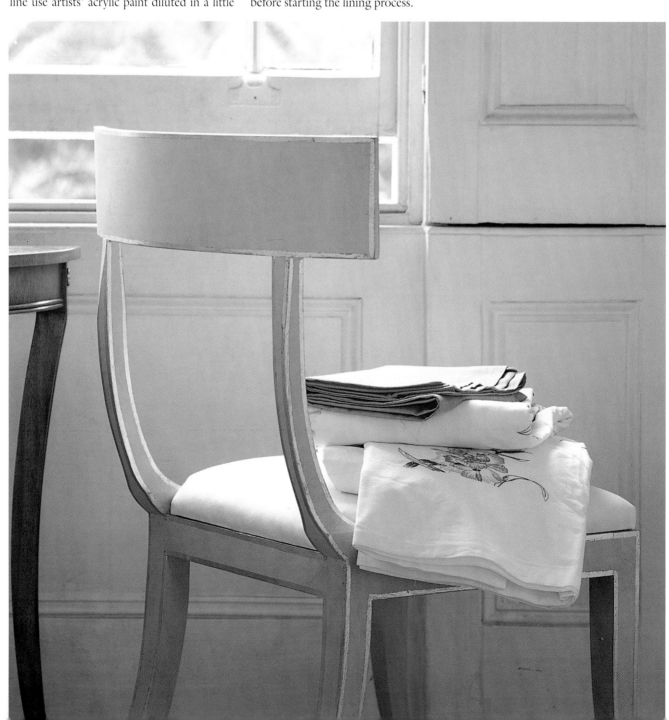

1 **Preparing the base** Prepare the base as described. Place the item at a convenient height so you can comfortably reach the area you are lining. Plan your order of painting so you won't smudge a line trying to reach across it.

2 **Mixing the paint** In a jar mix your choice of paint to a creamy consistency with the appropriate thinner. Add a dash of clear water- or oil-based varnish to improve the flow of the paint. Practise lining on the edge of scrap board or paper. Adjust the paint consistency if necessary.

3 **Adding guide marks (optional)** Decide on the distance between the edge of the item and the line, or the width of the lining. Cut a notch in a piece of cardboard to this distance. Draw the notched card around the edge of the item, marking the lining position with tiny dots of paint.

4 **Positioning the brush** Dip the lining brush in the paint and remove any excess on the side of the jar. Holding the brush towards the end of its handle, stand back from the surface so that you can comfortably reach it with your arm extended.

5 **Painting the lines** With a swift, relaxed movement and even pressure, start drawing the line – it may help to steady your hand by resting your little finger against the edge of the item. Keep the brush moving even if it wobbles – you can correct mistakes later. Keep your eye slightly ahead of the brush, and trust that your hand will follow. Try to paint each line in one go, otherwise overlap the ends and remove any excess paint later.

6 **Making corrections** Correct mistakes when you've completed a line while the paint is still wet. Use a cotton ball moistened with water or white spirit to wipe off imperfections. If the paint is already dry, rub it off very carefully with fine grade wet and dry paper and paint again if necessary.

7 **Retouching** Continue lining until the decoration is complete, then allow to dry. Retouch any lines if necessary, using a very light hand to avoid any variations in colour, especially with water-based paints. Allow to dry.

8 **Varnishing** If you want to give a worn, antique look to the line, rub lightly with fine grade abrasive paper. Apply a coat of matt or semi-gloss clear polyurethane varnish or a crackle-effect varnish. Allow to dry.

◄ *A basic wooden chair becomes part of a grander scheme with the addition of golden contours painted along the edges.*

Traditional lining patterns often take a twist at corners in the form of box or arc shapes.

Square corners To paint a box pattern – facing inwards (top) or outwards (bottom) – plan the shape carefully so it looks balanced, then mark each corner with a dot of paint. Join up the dots with fine lines.

Arc corners To paint an arc, position your little finger at the corner of the item and pivot your hand and the brush about this point. Practise on scrap board first until you're confident of the action.

▶ *The simple decoration of a fine white line gives a crisp edge and elegant air to an occasional table.*

LINING TRICKS

Applying a barrier coat of varnish before you start lining is the simplest way to achieve good results because you can easily wipe away any errors. If you're still a little uncertain, consider using one of the lining tricks that even some professional decorators resort to. Select the appropriate tools from the lists on this and the previous pages. Rub-down lettering transfers, which include lines, are available from art shops.

Painting adjacent dark and light lines – suggesting shady or lit areas – gives the convincing impression of moulding around each panel of this wardrobe.

YOU WILL NEED

- ❖ RULER/STRAIGHTEDGE
- ❖ CORKS and ADHESIVE
- ❖ CHALK or SOFT PENCIL
- ❖ MASKING TAPE and CRAFT KNIFE
- ❖ FELT-TIP PEN
- ❖ RUB-DOWN TRANSFER LINES

Using a ruler or straightedge For fairly short straight lines, place a ruler, bevelled side down, along the proposed line. For longer straight lines, stick corks to the underside of a straightedge to hold it away from the surface. Resting your middle finger against the edge of the ruler or straightedge, draw the brush across the surface.

Marking a guideline Use chalk or a soft pencil to draw faint lines, ruled or freehand, over the surface. These provide a painting guide and allow you to judge the best position for the lining. Remove any chalk dust before painting.

Masking straight lines Masking tape provides a useful guide for straight lines. As the tape can pull off the paint, apply a barrier coat of varnish first. Stick the tape so it masks one or both sides of the line. Press firmly along the tape to make sure paint can't seep underneath then paint along the tape edge. Peel off the tape immediately after painting each section to keep a clean edge.

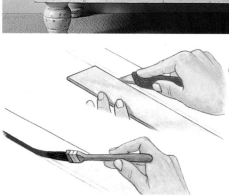

Using felt-tip pens You may find a felt-tip pen easier to control than a brush. Use a water-resistant type with a suitable width nib – metallic pens are particularly effective. After lining, apply a finishing coat of varnish and the result will look almost the same as hand-painted lines.

Scoring straight lines
Using a straightedge and a sharp-bladed craft knife, lightly score two parallel lines at the required position and width of the lining. Draw the brush very carefully between the lines, which should help to contain the paint.

Using transfers
Manufacturers of rub-down lettering also produce lines of varying widths, which you can use for straight lines – curve them carefully around corners. Finish with a coat of varnish for durable results.

POTS OF COLOUR

Turn plain terracotta pots into lively accessories by painting them with bold colours and geometric patterns. The pots are inexpensive and any shape or size is suitable for painting.

I t's fun and easy to brighten up plain terracotta pots with painted patterns. Stick to painting large areas of colour in cheerful designs, such as stripes, spots, zigzags or checks, that are simple enough to work freehand. If you're after a neater, straight-line look, use masking tape to create regular bands of vivid colour.

The surface of the terracotta takes paint well – matt vinyl emulsion (flat latex) is ideal. You'll need a smallish decorator's brush for putting on the base coat and a medium size round artist's brush for applying small patterns or fine details. A flat artist's or decorator's brush is best for painting stripes – choose one to match the width of stripe you want to paint.

Inexpensive terracotta pots come in a range of sizes from garden centres and do-it-yourself stores. Planted or left outside, painted pots will weather naturally to a softer, slightly faded look. If you want to slow this process down, line the pot with plastic before planting, making a hole in the base for drainage. When you're leaving your pots outside and want the colours to stay bright, use special masonry paint instead of interior emulsion (latex).

Why not paint a series of pots in coordinating colours for a bold display? The colours used here were royal blue, fuchsia pink, yellow and emerald.

PAINTING A POT

Before you begin to paint, empty any pots that have already been used for plants and check for mould. If you find mould, clear it away with a fungicide and then scrub the pot thoroughly in warm, soapy water. Rinse and allow it to dry completely before applying any paint.

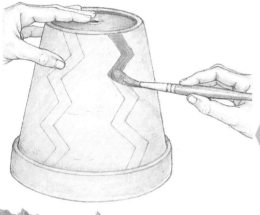

Painting the base colour
Apply a coat of the base colour, inside and out, and allow to dry. For a denser colour, apply two more coats, allowing the paint to dry between coats.

Painting zigzags Turn the pot upside down. Lightly pencil in the zigzag lines, each one going from the top to the base of the pot. Using an artist's brush, carefully paint in the zigzags.

Painting stripes Paint these freehand, letting the width of the paint brush determine the stripe. Alternatively for regular stripes, mask off the areas that are to be left in the base colour. Paint on a second colour, allow the paint to dry, then remove the masking tape.

Painting spots For perfectly round spots, cut a circle of the required spot size from cardboard, or use a round object such as a coin. Stick this to the pot with Blu-Tack. Lightly draw round the circle with a pencil. Repeat to draw all the spots you need, then carefully paint them in using a round artist's brush.

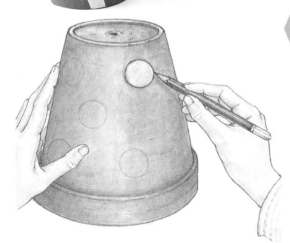

TIP

PAINTING THE RIM

For extra decoration, you can leave the rim of the pot plain or paint it in a different colour or pattern – a pink zigzag edging adds a charming contrast trim to the little white and blue spotted pot on the right.

Painting China and Glass

Try hand-painting china and glass to create unique decorative objects for your home.

You can use the wide range of craft paints now on the market to turn everyday china and glass items into ornamental pieces that add character and style to your home. Since you must never let the decorated surfaces come into contact with cutlery, food or the mouth, as many of the paints are toxic, and because the finishes are delicate, many hand-painted items are best used for display purposes only. When it comes to cleaning, most should be just wiped over with a damp cloth. Check the manufacturer's instructions on the paint you are using for practical guidance.

Suitable items

You can decorate both glazed and unglazed china or pottery items with paints, including vases, jugs, plant pots, candlesticks, tiles and crockery. Plain, white china pieces, commonly known as blanks, are particularly suitable, as the painted colours look brighter and clearer on pale backgrounds. Embossed surfaces work well if you incorporate the raised pattern into your painted design.

You can also paint all manner of glass objects – jugs, glasses, decanters, mirrors and vases look attractive decorated with opaque or transparent paint. You can even create a stained-glass effect at windows to screen and add colour to a room.

Choosing paints

Apart from ceramic and glass paints, you can use artists' materials and household and car paints as well. Craft shops and art stores sell craft paints in kit form, which is helpful for beginners.

Water-based paints tend to be a more practical choice than solvent-based paints as they are easier to apply and correct, and you can also clean the brushes with water.

Ceramic paints

These opaque paints are usually divided into two groups:

Cold ceramic paints are solvent-based and left to dry naturally. Most take about 24 hours to harden, although some alkyd resin paints only take about 3 hours. They dry with a glossy enamel-like finish; you get a more transparent effect by thinning the paint with a special colourless extender. The paints that take longer to dry are usually coated with varnish to make them more resilient. Most paint manufacturers provide compatible varnishes for you to use.

Heat-hardened ceramic paints Most water-based ceramic paints dry in about 4 hours but then need to be hardened in an oven for about 30 minutes. The resulting glossy finish is quite tough; you can wash it by hand in warm water with a mild detergent, but do not leave it to soak.

Acrylic paints

Acrylic paints come in an excellent range of bright colours with matt and shiny finishes. Strictly speaking, they are artists' paints, but work well on both china and glass. Extremely versatile, acrylic paints are easy to apply and are quick-drying.

Enamel paints

Available in matt and gloss finishes, enamel paints give smooth, hardwearing cover. They are usually solvent-based, but water-based products are now available.

Spray paints

Particularly good for stencilled effects, spray paints are easy to use and create a smooth finish in both gloss and matt finishes. They tend to be quite expensive, as there is a lot of wastage, and the fumes are unpleasant. Car spray paints are useful for metallic colours; otherwise use household or model paint sprays.

Glass paints

Transparent and opaque paints designed for painting on glass are available in both solvent-based and water-based forms. The water-based glass paints are excellent for children to work with as they dry quickly. The transparent types are very concentrated and good for creating a stained-glass effect; a special outlining paste is used to separate the colours and to simulate the leading of authentic stained glass.

On china, transparent glass paints produce a translucent finish; a colourless extender is added to make paler shades.

Useful equipment

Chinagraph pencil These wax pencils are useful for drawing on glass or china as the lines wipe off easily.
Cotton buds Good for creating a softly dotted pattern.
Craft knife Used for cutting out stencils.
Masking tape Useful for painting crisp, straight lines and for holding stencils in place. Cut low-tack tape into shapes for reversed out stencil motifs or patterns.
Paint brushes Use soft-bristled artists' or craft brushes. Choose a size to suit the job – the smaller the area, the smaller the brush you require.
Sponges Small pieces of natural sponge create delicate sponged effects. Crumpled tissue paper produces a sharper, straight-edged yet still random effect.

opaque glass paint
enamel paint
acrylic paint
glass paints
metallic spray paint
chinagraph pencil

acrylic paint
enamel paint
ceramic paint
ceramic paint
metallic ceramic paint
metallic spray paint

Using the paints

Always read the manufacturer's instructions before you start painting as some paints contain toxic substances and need careful handling. To be on the safe side, do not paint surfaces that will come into contact with food or the mouth, even if the paint is labelled non-toxic.

You can mix paints to create different shades, but you must stick to the same type of paint. To thin down paint and clean brushes, always use a compatible thinner – for solvent-based paints, use the special solvent thinner supplied by the paint manufacturers, or use turpentine or white/mineral spirit; for water-based paints use water.

Bear in mind that unglazed or porous surfaces, such as terracotta, absorb paints and make the colour look darker, unless you seal the surface first with an appropriate undercoat.

Most craft paint finishes are fairly delicate and often require a final coating of varnish to help protect the design. Special glazes are usually sold with each different brand of paint.

Preparation

You must clean all surfaces thoroughly before painting them. Wash both ceramics and glass with soapy water, rinse and dry; use methylated spirits to remove any stubborn grease.

Practise the different painting techniques on scraps of paper before you start, to give yourself confidence and to help you decide which technique and design you want to use. If you are planning a detailed design, measure up the area you want to paint to get an idea of the scale, then draw the design on paper. For freehand painting on china, use the drawing as a reference. If you are not confident about painting directly on to the china use a chinagraph pencil to draw on the outlines of the design before you begin to apply the paints.

On transparent glass, tape the drawing behind the glass or put it inside the vessel and hold it tightly against the surface with wads of old newspaper. You can then follow the drawn pattern as you paint on the outside of the vessel.

Techniques

The following techniques will help you to achieve professional-looking results.

Straight lines

To paint a straight edge or to create thick lines, press strips of masking tape on to the surface to be decorated. Paint the unmasked area and when the paint is nearly dry, remove the tape.

Masking off

Cut out shapes from low-tack masking tape and fix them on to the surface. Use a brush to apply glass or ceramic paint all over the surface. Alternatively, hold a can of spray paint about 30cm (1ft) from the surface and spray with even movements from side to side. Remove the stick-on shapes when the paint is touch-dry.

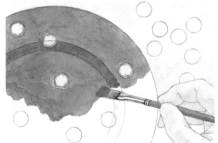

Sponging

Dip a small piece of sponge into a saucer of paint, remove excess paint by dabbing the sponge on to newspaper, then dab it on to the surface in a random pattern. Vary the pressure and the spacing to achieve different effects. Experiment with more than one colour but allow the first colour to dry before you apply the second.

Stained-glass effect

1 **Drawing the design** Draw or trace the 'leading' design on to the surface, then apply the outliner by pressing on the tube with the tip just touching the surface. Allow to dry.

2 **Painting in the colour** Fill in the sections with a generous amount of paint, blending the paint as well as possible to prevent the brush marks from showing.

Resist painting

1 **Drawing the design** Using a chinagraph pencil, draw the outline of the design on to the surface. Fill in any areas you want to remain as the original background with chinagraph.

2 **Painting the design** Paint in the design with ceramic paints, using a fine brush for line work and a rounder one for solid areas. When all the paint is dry, rub off the chinagraph with a soft, dry cloth to reveal the original background underneath.

TRADITIONAL DECOUPAGE

With traditional decoupage, paper motifs are glued to an object and varnished until they appear to be part of the surface. It is not a difficult craft and one that, with a little patience, can be extremely rewarding.

Decoupage is one of the most satisfying ways to add character to plain accessories. A major attraction is that the basic technique is so straightforward, requiring little in the way of specialist or costly equipment. Arm yourself with a pair of sharp nail scissors, printed paper, adhesive and varnish, find an object to decorate – and you're ready to start.

For your first project it is best to decorate something small with a flat surface – an inexpensive trinket box is ideal. Rummage around at home, or look in secondhand shops for a suitable item. Its condition doesn't matter as it can be painted and the decoupage itself hides any imperfections. If you buy a new item, plain objects made in wood or MDF (medium density fibreboard) are inexpensive and perfectly suitable.

The real skill in decoupage lies in selecting paper motifs that flatter and are in keeping with the character and shape of the object being decorated. When you are decorating a new item, choose paint (if you're using it) and papers in colours and themes to coordinate with other furnishings in the room where it will be displayed. With older items choose motifs that are sympathetic to the period and style of the piece itself.

The decoration can be quite minimal – a single motif strategically placed can be very effective – or it can be more involved, with a number of motifs grouped so that some of the background shows through. Alternatively, the entire surface can be covered with a collage of motifs, so that none of the background is visible – an option worth considering if the object is damaged.

A new pine tray looks like a desirable antique after being covered with a brilliant decoupage design. The tray was first stained to make it seem well aged, then decorated with lush fruit motifs which were cut from gift wrap and outlined in gold metallic pen.

DECORATING WITH DECOUPAGE

When building up layers of paint, paper and varnish on a box it is important to check that the lid still fits. Ideally start with a lid that is a little loose, or make sure that you do not add too many layers to the inside of the lid and upper inside edges of the box.

For your first project, choose a small wooden item with a smooth, flat surface such as a box or tray. The wood should be bare – remove any existing varnish at the start and fill all the cracks with a fine-surface filler. Rub down rough edges or surfaces with fine sandpaper, brush the resulting dust away and wipe the surface down with a damp cloth to clean it, making it easier to work with.

If the wood has an attractive grain, you may decide to stick the motifs straight on to the surface. Or you can stain or paint it in a colour which looks good with your chosen motifs – use emulsion (latex) or acrylic paint or a water-based stain.

CHOOSING PAPERS

The Victorians used specially printed motifs of flowers and fruit, butterflies and cherubs called decals for their decoupage decorations. You can buy similar images in sheet form from bookshops, craft shops and museums.

Giftwrapping paper is another good source of decoupage motifs. Most papers with a matt finish work well, provided they are printed on one side only, as any print on the underside tends to show through after gluing. Avoid foil wrapping paper, since it is difficult to lay flat without creasing.

You could also experiment with wallpapers, magazines, labels, tickets, stamps or photocopied pictures from books as alternative sources of motifs. If you want to use photocopies or paint your own motifs, you need to seal them first with a diluted PVA solution. Mix one measure of glue into two equal measures of water and brush this over the surface of the motif. Allow it to dry before gluing to the object.

Look for designs which have a variety of clearly identifiable shapes in a range of shades or colours. Motifs from different papers can be combined in one design as long as the papers are of a similar thickness.

SEALING THE DESIGN

Once you have stuck on the motifs and left them to dry, varnish the surface to protect it and give a smooth finish. Use a matt or satin water-based varnish. Several coats of matt varnish have a subtle sheen whereas two or three coats of satin varnish look quite shiny.

DECORATING A SMALL BOX

The trinket box used here is made of MDF (medium density fibreboard). Before painting or applying decoupage motifs to bare MDF, you need to seal the surface with a coat of diluted PVA or undercoat to hold down any stray fibres. Once the sealant has dried, paint it to coordinate with the motifs. Water-based matt emulsion or acrylic paint is ideal.

After sticking on the motifs, varnish as for wood.

YOU WILL NEED

- ❖ GIFTWRAP or other sort of paper with your choice of motifs
- ❖ Large sharp SCISSORS
- ❖ Small sharp SCISSORS
- ❖ PAPER and PENCIL
- ❖ PVA ADHESIVE
- ❖ Two small PAINT BRUSHES
- ❖ KITCHEN PAPER TOWEL or SPONGE
- ❖ WALLPAPER SEAM ROLLER (optional)
- ❖ CLEAR WATER-BASED VARNISH in a MATT or SATIN FINISH
- ❖ FINE GLASSPAPER/SAND PAPER
- ❖ NEUTRAL FURNITURE WAX

1 Cutting out the motifs Using large scissors, roughly cut out motifs from the giftwrap. With the smaller scissors trim the motifs precisely to get a smooth, even outline. Hold the small scissors at a slight inward angle to bevel the edge so that the motif lies flat on the surface when stuck down.

4 Completing the design Following your design plan, apply more motifs in the same way until you have covered the lid and decorated the sides of the box. Ensure that the finished surface is completely flat and even. Leave to dry overnight.

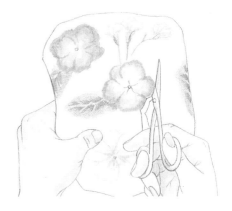

2 Working out the design Draw round the lid on a piece of plain paper and lay out the motifs within the outline. Try overlapping some of the shapes and leaving a little plain background showing between others.

3 Sticking down the first motif If the PVA is very thick, dilute it to the consistency of thin cream. Using a small, clean paint brush, carefully brush PVA over the back of the first motif and position it on the box lid. Press it down firmly with a sheet of kitchen towel or a sponge, making sure that there are no bubbles under the motif. If you have a wallpaper seam roller, roll it gently over the edges.

5 Varnishing over the motifs Apply a thin coat of varnish over the decoupaged surface with a soft brush. Allow the varnish to dry, then rub over lightly using fine glasspaper/sandpaper. Repeat twice to apply a total of three coats. For a smoother finish apply more coats of varnish and let dry.

TIP

COVERING THE BASE

To neaten the base of your box or tray, cut a piece of coloured felt to fit and glue it on.

Daffodils cut from a sheet of gift wrap are stuck straight on to the wood, giving this little box a charming fresh appeal.

6 Adding finishing touches For a rich finish, apply a coat of neutral furniture wax over the surface of your decoupaged object. Buff to a deep shine.

DECOUPAGE IDEAS

Decoupage works well on rounded surfaces as well as flat ones. You can also try it on different surface materials such as metals or ceramics. Flowerpots, candlesticks and picture frames with smooth, curved sides are particularly appropriate for decorating with motifs.

Prime metal surfaces with quick-drying metal primer before painting with a solvent-based undercoat and two coats of solvent-based satin sheen paint.

Before painting, terracotta needs to be sealed with a commercial water sealer. You don't need any special preparation for china – just brush on acrylic, emulsion or ceramic paint, or decoupage straight on to the surface.

For metal and ceramic surfaces, use PVA adhesive to stick on the motifs, following the steps on the previous pages. On metal and over solvent-based paints, use polyurethane varnish, which you must leave to dry overnight. Plastic items or those with highly sealed finishes are unsuitable for decoupage as the paint and adhesive do not stick well.

▲ *Floral decoupage completely transforms a plain tray. Two large motifs depicting bouquets of roses form the basis of the design with smaller posies lined up about them to form a frame.*

▶ *A flower-strewn decoupage motif enhances a display of cut flowers or a pot of flowering plants. When adding motifs to a planted pot, keep the decoupage about 2cm (¾in) above the base so water doesn't damage it. It's also a good idea to seal the inside of the pot with a coat of proprietary water sealer.*

▲ *This pink-painted photo frame is decorated with a romantic rose motif. The roses tumble on to the glass of the frame to provide the ideal setting for a single cherub.*

◀ *An old plate was first painted with emulsion then decorated with distinctive motifs of fans. The plate can only be used for display purposes.*

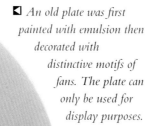

◀ *Victorian-style decoupage motifs are usually printed in sheet form, following a theme. Here single cherub motifs add decorative interest to two plain candlesticks.*

Glass Decoupage

Transform a plain glass vase into a beautiful accessory
for your home by pasting cut-out paper motifs to the inside, then painting the
background in a complementary colour.

All kinds of everyday glass objects, from plain kitchen plates and bowls to shapely vases, dishes and lampbases, can easily be given a completely new finish with decoupage motifs. Decoupage is a simple technique – the word comes from the French word *découper*, meaning to cut out; decoupage means the process of decorating a surface with cut-out motifs. With glass decoupage, the paper cutouts are stuck to the inside of the glass with a clear adhesive, before the whole interior of the vessel is covered with paint. This is followed with a layer of varnish to seal the design.

Decoupaged glass items cannot be used to hold liquids but make good containers for dried flowers or foliage, as well as being attractive accessories in their own right. If you want to display fresh flowers in a decoupaged vase, stand another water-tight container inside it first and arrange the flowers in that.

Gift wrapping paper was the low-cost starting point for these two pretty vases in matching blue and yellow. Themed motifs like stars can be used to create a coordinated collection of decoupage glassware.

101

DECOUPAGE GLASS VASE

YOU WILL NEED
- ❖ PAPER MOTIFS
- ❖ POINTED SCISSORS
- ❖ SPRAY FIXATIVE
- ❖ GLASS VASE
- ❖ BLU-TACK
- ❖ CHINAGRAPH CRAYON
- ❖ PVA ADHESIVE
- ❖ SMALL PAINT BRUSH
- ❖ DAMP CLOTH
- ❖ WATER-BASED PAINT
- ❖ SMALL SPONGE
- ❖ CLEAR WATER-BASED VARNISH

Part of the fun of decoupage lies in finding the motifs. Giftwrap, wallpaper, magazines and photocopies are all good sources. Choose strong papers, rather than tissue or other delicate types, which will withstand wetting by adhesive and paint without tearing or disintegrating. Also look for well defined motifs that are easy to cut out. Choose glass with a smooth surface. The neck should be wide enough to allow your hand inside to apply cut-out motifs and to paint and varnish the inside.

The technique is simple. The cut-out motifs are sprayed with fixative to stop them becoming transparent when wet. They are then arranged on the outside of the vase and their positions marked on the glass with a chinagraph crayon (available from art shops); this can be rubbed off later. The motifs are stuck to the inside with PVA adhesive, which is white when applied but dries clear.

Finally the inside of the vase is painted with water based paint – artist's acrylics, emulsion or children's poster paints are all suitable – and sealed with a coat of clear varnish.

1 Sealing the motifs Cut out motifs and spray the wrong sides with fixative. When they are dry, experiment with the position of your motifs by arranging them on the outside of the vase, using Blu-Tack to hold them in place temporarily.

2 Marking motif positions If you are using several cutouts, mark their positions on the outside of the glass by drawing round them with a chinagraph crayon to help reposition them on the inside. The crayon can be wiped off once the motifs are in place.

3 Sticking the cutouts Apply a coat of adhesive to the right side of a motif and position it inside the vase. Smooth cutout flat with a slightly dampened cloth. Stick other motifs in the same way. Allow them to dry. Wipe off the crayon marks with a damp cloth.

TIP
COLOUR CHECK
Before sticking the motifs, check the effect against your background colour by placing a piece of paper painted in the same colour inside the vase.

▶ *After lining a glass vase with motifs cut from a sheet of floral gift wrap, paint on a backing colour that sets them off to perfection.*

4 Painting the background Use the sponge to dab an even coat of paint over the inside of the vase. Leave to dry before applying a second coat. Apply more layers until the colour looks evenly opaque. When dry, brush a thin coat of varnish over the inside of the vase and leave to dry.

CURVED GLASS DECOUPAGE

Glass vessels are a wonderful base for decoupage – their curved surfaces provide a smooth clear base for the cutout paper motifs.

With decoupage, one way to develop a realistic sense of depth and movement in the design is to use a base item with a curved surface. Without having to accommodate corners and angles, you can arrange the cutout motifs so they flow naturally around the item. The organic nature of glass – blown or moulded into curvaceous shapes – lends itself particularly well to this type of decoupage design.

In glass decoupage you stick the motifs face down to the inside or underside of the item and view them through the glass. The notion of being behind glass gives the decoupage a precious quality and also acts to magnify the colour and detail of the motifs. Traditional decoupage is painted with several coats of varnish, giving it a smooth lacquer-like finish, but with glass decoupage the deep polished surface is ready-made.

When choosing an item to decoupage, remember that you won't be able to immerse it in water after decorating it. A purely decorative item, such as a lampbase, fruit bowl or cake stand that you can wipe clean, makes a perfect base. Items with shallow curved surfaces make it easier to stick the motifs smoothly in place. Don't use textured glass because you won't be able to see the motifs through it.

A platter is a simple starting point for glass decoupage, as its shallow curve makes arranging and sticking the motifs fairly straightforward.

Decoupage on a curved glass surface uses similar techniques to that on flat surfaces; it's just a little trickier to stick the motifs so they lie smooth.

CHOOSING MOTIFS

If the glass has a curved surface, like this vase, creases and bubbles are difficult to avoid. The best solution to the problem is to choose small motifs. Intricately patterned motifs also help to hide creases. A mediumweight paper, such as gift wrap, is easier to work with as it's neither too stiff to shape nor so fragile that it tears. Also once you moisten the paper with glue, it softens a little, making it easier to smooth into place.

If you think an obvious crease or bubble is going to form, make a cut into the motif, along a shape or line in its pattern, and slide the paper over itself so it fits the curved surface. Creases and cuts in large or plain motifs would be too noticeable – so consider this when choosing your motifs.

Patience is the best policy – take time to smooth each motif gently into place so it doesn't tear. If the motifs overlap, allow time for the glue to dry before sticking another motif on top, otherwise an inaccessible bubble may form on a lower layer.

PLACING THE MOTIFS

Rather than placing the motifs randomly over the base – which tends to flatten both the object and design – try to link the motifs to each other and to the shape of the glass. With careful arrangement you can create a sense of depth or movement in the design. Consider the subject matter and arrange it accordingly – so a bird doesn't look as if it's about to crash land or a bouquet of flowers take flight.

YOU WILL NEED

- ❖ GLASS VASE or PLATTER
- ❖ SMALL SHARP SCISSORS
- ❖ PAPER MOTIFS
- ❖ SPRAY FIXATIVE
- ❖ BLU-TACK
- ❖ CHINAGRAPH CRAYON
- ❖ PVA ADHESIVE
- ❖ SMALL PAINT BRUSH
- ❖ SMALL SPONGE, CLOTHS
- ❖ WATER-BASED PAINT
- ❖ CLEAR WATER-BASED VARNISH

1 Preparing the base Make sure the glass base is perfectly clean and dust-free. If necessary wash out the base with soapy water to remove any stains, then rinse and dry it.

2 Sealing the motifs Use the small scissors to cut out the motifs. Spray the wrong side of the motifs with fixative to stop them becoming transparent when varnished. Allow to dry.

3 Arranging the motifs Arrange the motifs round the inside of the base, holding them in place with Blu-Tack. Link them to the base shape and to each other to give the image a sense of depth.

4 Fitting motifs on a curved surface One by one press the motifs gently against the glass. If you think a crease may form, remove the motif and cut short slits into it, following the shapes and lines of its pattern. Reposition the motif on the base, overlapping the paper at the slits so that it fits the curved surface. Make further slits if necessary until the motif lies smoothly on the surface.

5 Marking the design Use a chinagraph crayon to mark the outline of the motifs on the outside of the glass. Gently remove all the motifs from the base.

6 Sticking the motifs Dilute the PVA adhesive with water so that it is the consistency of single cream. Apply a thin, even coat to the right side of a motif. Using the crayon marks as a guide, position the motif on the inside of the glass base. Overlap any cuts you made in the motif so it lies smooth. Using a slightly damp cloth, gently yet firmly rub over the motif to remove any air bubbles. If decorating the underside of an item, such as a platter, lift it up occasionally to check the motifs from the right side. Apply the remaining motifs and allow them to dry.

7 Painting the background Wipe off the crayon marks with a damp cloth. Paint the inside of the base with a sponge, dabbing the paint on to avoid tearing the motifs. Use a clean damp cloth to remove any excess paint round the rim. Leave the paint to dry, then apply further coats until the colour is even, letting each coat dry and wiping the rim each time. When the final coat is dry, apply thin coats of varnish over it.

The flowers decorating this glass vase sweep around its sides reflecting the natural growth of the stems and the simple arrangement of flowers within the vase. Standing another container inside the decoupaged vase to hold fresh flowers prevents the design getting wet.

DECOUPAGE LAMPBASE

YOU WILL NEED

- ❖ MATERIALS FOR CURVED DECOUPAGE
- ❖ VESSEL FOR LAMPBASE
- ❖ ONE LAMP KIT consisting of adaptor bung to fit base, brass bulb holder and three-core flex/cord
- ❖ ADJUSTABLE SPANNER
- ❖ SHARP TRIMMING KNIFE
- ❖ WIRE STRIPPERS
- ❖ THREE-PIN PLUG
- ❖ 3A FUSE

For a decoupage lampbase you can use a vase, goldfish bowl or storage jar, as long as its neck is wide enough for your hand to fit through. As this lampbase has straight sides, you don't need to cut any slits in the motifs to ease them round the shape.

In addition to the equipment needed for glass decoupage you need a lamp kit to convert the base into a lampbase. These are available from larger lighting stockists, from craft stores or by mail order.

1 **Sticking the decoupage** Following steps 1-7, *Curved Decoupage*, arrange and stick the motifs round the inside of the base. Paint and varnish inside.

2 **Threading the flex** If the glass base has a hole at the bottom for the flex, run the flex through the hole, up through the neck of the base (**A**) and through the central stud of the adaptor bung. If the base does not have a hole for the flex, thread the flex through the side hole in the central stud (**B**). Place the bung into the neck of the lampbase. Holding it firmly, use an adjustable spanner to tighten the nut at the base of the bung stud.

Choose a particular theme for the image and link the motifs to each other. These Victorian ladies look as if they are promenading beside a colourful flower border.

3 **Preparing the flex** Dismantle the brass bulb holder. Thread the flex through the base of the bulb holder and screw on to the adaptor stud. Use a trimming knife to cut back about 2.5cm (1in) of the outer flex insulation. Use wire strippers to trim off about 1.2cm (½in) of insulation from the three wires. Twist the exposed strands of wire and bend them over to double thickness.

4 **Connecting the wires** To connect each wire, push the strands into a terminal and tighten the screw. Connect the brown wire to one of the two terminals in the bulb holder body and the blue wire to the other terminal in the bulb holder body. Connect the green and yellow wire to the earth terminal in the base of the bulb holder.

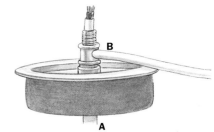

5 **Re-assembling the bulb holder** Push the bulb holder body into its base, at the same time gently drawing the flex back through the adaptor stud. Screw down the lower ridged ring to secure it. Fit the lampshade and bulb. Wire the other end of the flex to a three-pin plug and fit a 3A fuse.

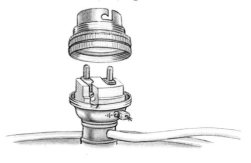

DECOUPAGE FIRESCREEN

*Make your own firescreen from inexpensive MDF and decorate
it with decoupage to suit your room exactly – the result is a wonderful
fireside accessory that would be very costly to buy.*

Once the warm glow of an open fire disappears, a fireplace can look rather cold and dark. Making and decorating a firescreen to place in front of the grate cheers up the whole hearth. It also means you can hide the grate if you haven't had time to reset the fire.

Decoupage is a traditional technique for decorating firescreens. Floral, bird and animal themes are the most popular styles but, with the enormous selection of decorative giftwrap available, the possibilities for other themes are almost limitless. Rather than going out with a particular design in mind, you're likely to have more success if you take your inspiration from the giftwrap you see – look for colours and themes that fit with the room scheme. By playing around with the motifs and perhaps combining a few different giftwrap designs, you can create your own unique decoupage pattern.

Make the firescreen and its stand from medium density fibreboard (MDF), which you cut to whatever size and shape you want. The simplest shapes are rectangular or square, cut using a panel saw. Traditionally though, decoupage firescreens are cut in a novelty shape that follows the outline of the decoupage design, using an electric jigsaw or coping saw. If you have not had much experience using a jigsaw, choose a shape without too many awkward corners to cut around and practise on a scrap piece of MDF first.

An imposing rectangular firescreen decorated with golden suns and stars, cut from sheets of giftwrap, gives this fireplace a fiery cheer even when the grate is cold and empty.

MAKING A SHAPED FIRESCREEN

YOU WILL NEED

- ❖ 6mm (¼in) thick sheet of MDF for the firescreen
- ❖ 15mm (⅝in) thick sheet of MDF for the firescreen stand
- ❖ 2 OR 3 SHEETS OF GIFTWRAP
- ❖ LARGE and SMALL SHARP SCISSORS
- ❖ PENCIL
- ❖ TRACING PAPER
- ❖ LOW-ADHESIVE STICKY TAPE
- ❖ ELECTRIC JIGSAW or COPING SAW
- ❖ DRILL and DRILL BIT
- ❖ FINE GLASSPAPER/SAND PAPER
- ❖ 40mm (1½in) and 12mm (½in) PAINT BRUSHES
- ❖ WATER-BASED PRIMER
- ❖ ACRYLIC PAINT
- ❖ PVA ADHESIVE
- ❖ POLYURETHANE VARNISH in a matt or satin finish
- ❖ BUTTERFLY HINGES

The size of firescreen you make is up to you, as long as it's large enough to hide the grate. If you are making a shaped screen, try to arrange the motifs in a symmetrical shape so they look balanced.

Don't be too hasty about cutting into the giftwrap – lay out the sheets and look at their overall designs first. Overlap them to see how the motifs and colours fit together. To create a three-dimensional effect with a sense of perspective, build up the design using smaller scale motifs first and then overlaying the larger scale pieces on top. Don't worry about leaving gaps in-between the cutouts, as the plain painted background provides relief against a busy pattern.

1 Planning the design Decide which motifs you want to use and how to arrange them. Carefully cut out the motifs, using small scissors for more intricate shapes. Arrange the cutouts on a flat surface and adjust their positions until you are pleased with the result. Lay a sheet of tracing paper on top. Trace the design outline and the positions of the cutouts.

2 Measuring up for the MDF Measure the maximum length and width of the design adding 15cm (6in) to each measurement to allow for any adjustments. Buy or cut a rectangle of 6mm (¼in) thick MDF to these dimensions.

3 Cutting out the screen To make a template, cut along the outline of the firescreen design which you have drawn on the tracing paper. Lay the template on the MDF, using low-adhesive sticky tape to keep it in place. With a pencil draw around the template on to the MDF. Remove the template. Hold the MDF securely on a flat work surface so one section of the outline overhangs the edge. Using an electric jigsaw cut along the drawn outline of the overhanging section. Reposition the MDF to cut all round the outline and drill holes for inserting the jigsaw blade for internal cutouts as necessary. Sand the cut edges using fine glasspaper/sandpaper.

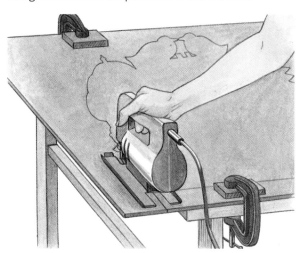

4 Painting the screen Paint the MDF all over with a water-based primer/undercoat. Apply two coats of acrylic paint using a small paint brush for the edges to avoid drips. Allow each coat time to dry before applying the next, but wash the brushes out straightaway.

5 Sticking the cutouts Using PVA adhesive, paste the cutouts in place, building up the design piece by piece following your tracing. Use a soft rag or sponge to smooth the cutouts, removing any air bubbles and pressing down the edges. Allow the adhesive to dry.

MAKING A STAND

1 **Cutting the stand pieces** Lay the firescreen face down and measure and mark a vertical line down the centre of the back. The stand height needs to be three-quarters the length of this line, so divide the length by four and multiply by three to find the stand height (**A**). Cut two pieces of 15mm (⅝in) thick MDF to the shapes in the diagram (below right), so their length equals **A**. Paint and varnish the stand pieces in the same way as for the screen.

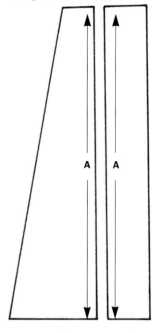

2 **Attaching the stand** Using PVA, stick the rectangular strip of MDF to the back of the firescreen, in line with the centre mark and the base edge. Weight the stand with heavy books until the PVA is dry.

◁ *Conjure up tales of eastern promise at the fireside. With such a wide variety of giftwrap designs available you can make a decoupage firescreen to suit almost any mood or theme imaginable.*

3 **Fixing the hinges** Place the screen flat against a wall and hold the remaining part of the stand with its perpendicular edge adjacent to the fixed piece. Place the open butterfly hinges so they overlap the two parts of the stand, 10cm (4in) from the top and bottom edges. Mark the screw holes then remove the hinges and start the screw holes with a bradawl. Screw the hinges in place.

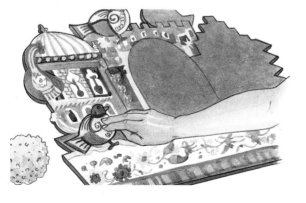

6 **Varnishing the screen** Apply a coat of polyurethane varnish over the screen with a soft paint brush. Allow the varnish to dry, then sand it lightly using dampened wet and dry paper. Varnish and sand again, then apply a final coat of varnish.

TIP
LARGE MOTIFS
Large pieces of giftwrap tend to crease or bubble when you stick them in place, so it is a good idea to cut them into smaller, more manageable pieces and butt-join them. To make the join less noticeable try to cut them out along a line in the motif design.

A rectangular firescreen is easier to cut out than a more elaborately shaped one, but looks just as effective when it's covered with a colourful mix of paper motifs. If you prefer, you can use another simple shape, like a triangle.

As an alternative to making a hinged stand at the back of the screen, make four feet cut from MDF and stick these to the lower edge of the screen.

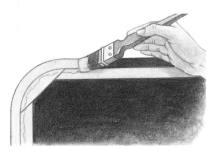

1 Cutting the screen Using a steel tape and set square mark a 600 x 700mm (23½ x 27½in) rectangle on to a sheet of 6mm (¼in) thick MDF. Round off the corners by drawing round an appropriately sized saucer at each corner. Secure the MDF to a flat work surface and use an electric jigsaw to cut around the marked outline. Also cut out a selection of paper motifs.

2 Cutting out the feet Choose one of the repeating motifs on the giftwrap – about 10cm (4in) wide – as the shape for the feet and cut out four. Place one on a piece of paper and draw around it leaving a 1.5cm (⅝in) border all round. Cut out the shape to make the foot template. Use the template to draw four feet shapes on to a piece of 18mm (¾in) thick MDF. Cut out the shapes using an electric jigsaw.

4 Painting the screen Prime and paint the board and feet following step 4, *Making a Shaped Firescreen*. Using low-adhesive sticky tape, mask all round the front edges of the screen, 1.5cm (⅝in) in from the edge. Paint a gold border all round the screen outside the masking tape. When the paint is dry, peel off the tape.

3 Attaching the feet Measure and mark 20cm (8in) in from both ends along the lower edge of the screen. Using PVA, stick two feet to the front of the screen so they centre over the marks and protrude 2.5cm (1in) below the lower edge of the screen. Allow the adhesive to dry and then stick the two remaining feet at the back of the screen exactly in line with the front feet.

5 Completing the screen Paste the motifs in place on the screen and feet and then varnish, following steps 5 and 6, *Making a Shaped Firescreen*.

◀ *Paint a piece of MDF with a colour that complements your chosen motifs, add a golden outline and then paste on the cutouts. If you decorate the front and back of the screen with different designs you just need to turn it round for an instant change of scene.*

MOULDINGS FOR CHARACTER

Use wooden moulded motifs to jazz up accessories and small pieces of furniture. Simply stick on the motifs, then paint the whole piece in the colours of your choice.

D ecorative wooden motifs can transform basic objects into eye-catching, original home accessories. You can use them to add character to featureless new objects such as plain trays or boxes, or to give a new lease of life to old items.

Buy your mouldings from home decorating stores or craft shops. Motifs vary from single flower and shell shapes to intricately detailed bows, rope-twist borders and flower-trimmed swags. The mouldings can be stuck on to any flat, clean surface which will support the weight. Use small light mouldings on lightweight surfaces

such as thick cardboard and tin, and light or heavier mouldings on wood, plaster, metal and plastic. If you choose a large moulding – 14cm (5½in) or bigger across – it is a good idea to use fine veneer pins for added strength when sticking it to a wooden surface.

Choose a paint finish to give a final touch of character to your decorated item. For a bright modern look, paint the moulding and the item in bold contrasting colours. Or use a paint effect such as sponging, or an antique finish like that illustrated on the last page of this feature.

Here wooden motifs have been painted white and applied to a blue cupboard, echoing the collection of Wedgwood pottery displayed above.

DESIGNING WITH MOTIFS

Choose motifs of a suitable size so that they look well balanced against the base object. Look for designs which complement the object you are decorating – if this is a bold shape with strong, straight lines choose a chunky motif rather than one with delicate curves.

Try out different effects by anchoring the motifs to the background with sticky tape or Blu-Tack. A single motif can be highlighted by placing curved mouldings on either side. This design looks particularly good on a drawer front, or you can use several curved mouldings to create an ornate classical-style picture frame.

If you are using several identical motifs, try arranging them side by side or in a chequered pattern to form a border around picture frames or trays, or group them centrally to decorate a cupboard door or the lid of a box.

▽ *Carved bows of all shapes and sizes are a marvellous way of adding a distinctive decoration to plain picture frames and boxes.*

DECORATING A UTENSIL BOX

Check that the surfaces of the base object and the motif are clean and dry before sticking on the moulding with a suitable adhesive. PVA wood adhesive was used for the wooden items illustrated here. Wherever possible, the work should be laid flat and the moulding taped or weighted down until the adhesive is dry.

To apply paint, a sponging technique is often more effective than using a paint brush as it produces a good overall depth of colour – use two different colours to create an interesting effect. If you want to paint the motif in a contrasting colour to the base object, sponge both separately before gluing on the motif – this method is described in the steps below.

If you are colour matching motif and base, it's best to glue on the motif before applying the colours over the entire piece.

◪ *After sponging the container with cream and yellow, and the motif with white and cream, the assembled piece was coated in varnish to give a durable finish.*

1 Preparing the surface
Rub down the wooden base surface with fine sandpaper and wipe away the dust. Prime any bare wood and leave to dry.

2 Painting the box
Using a sponge and your first choice of colour, dab paint over the box. Allow to dry then sponge on a second colour, letting some of the first colour show through. Leave to dry.

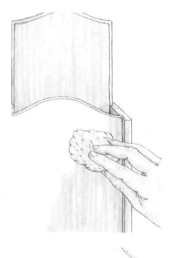

3 Painting the motif
Sponge your choice of colours over the motif, letting the paint dry thoroughly between coats.

TIP
USING A BRUSH
On intricately carved mouldings you may find a paint brush is more effective for applying paint than a sponge. Dip a dry, stiff bristled brush into the paint and dab it lightly into the recesses.

4 Sticking on the motif
Apply an even layer of adhesive to the back of the motif and press into position. Wipe away any excess adhesive. Hold the motif in place with masking tape and lay the object flat until dry.

5 Protecting the finish
Use a paint brush to apply two coats of varnish over the finished piece, allowing the varnish to dry between coats.

◪ *Highlighting the raised parts of the motif produces an attractive contrast between moulding and base. Either use a paint brush to apply a very light shade along the raised edge of the motif or sponge the dark shade over the whole motif and then wipe the colour away from the raised parts, leaving a little in the recesses of the motif.*

Decorating a Frame

An inexpensive wooden frame was the starting point for this lavish photograph frame complete with winged companions. Decorated with plastic cherubs and simple wooden motifs, it also has a raised inner edge made from uncooked spaghetti. Likely sources for plastic mouldings are home design shops – for cherubs, look in department stores before Christmas when they are sold as tree ornaments.

Once the trims are glued in position, the frame is given a mock gilded finish by applying gold paint over a rich base coat.

Remove the glass and backing board before working on the frame.

► *This cherubic frame has been aged by rubbing away some gold paint to reveal the rich colour underneath.*

You Will Need

❖ WIDE WOODEN FRAME

❖ WOODEN or PLASTIC MOULDINGS

❖ PVA WOOD ADHESIVE

❖ UNCOOKED SPAGHETTI

❖ WATER-BASED LATEX RUBBER ADHESIVE

❖ CRAFT KNIFE

❖ RED ACRYLIC PAINT

❖ PAINT BRUSH

❖ GOLD ACRYLIC PAINT

❖ COTTON CLOTHS

❖ WIRE WOOL (000 grade)

❖ DARK BEESWAX

1 Gluing on the mouldings Using wood adhesive, stick all of the mouldings in position on the frame. Cut the uncooked spaghetti to size and glue it in place with the latex rubber adhesive. Wipe off any excess adhesive and allow all adhesive to dry.

2 Colouring the frame Paint the frame and all the mouldings with two coats of red paint, allowing each to dry in between. Then paint on one coat of gold, covering all the red paint. Immediately wipe off a little of the gold paint with a cloth, to reveal streaks of red underneath. Allow to dry.

3 Ageing the frame Using a piece of fine wire wool, gently rub over the frame surface to distress it slightly. Then rub on dark beeswax with a clean cloth, rubbing off a little more of the gold paint in the process.

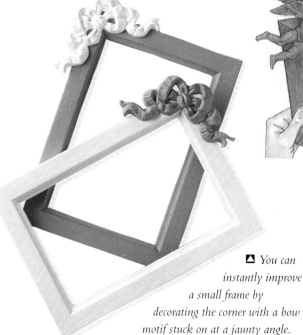

▲ *You can instantly improve a small frame by decorating the corner with a bow motif stuck on at a jaunty angle.*

PAPIER MACHE CONTAINERS

Decorative bowls and vases with impressive designer looks are yours for the making. Strip papier mâché, made from torn paper strips and glue, is a marvellous medium for expressing your creativity.

Modelling with papier mâché is a traditional craft that continues to fascinate designers because it is so versatile. You can work with papier mâché in various ways, and decorate it in a seemingly endless range of styles using a wide choice of materials.

Papier mâché is also very cheap to make. The basic ingredients are torn paper and glue and a suitable mould – almost any container or object with a shape you like will do. When the papier mâché has dried, you can either remove the

mould or leave it in place – to form a waterproof lining for a papier mâché vase, for example.

There are two main types of papier mâché – paper strip and pulp. You can make both kinds yourself, but if you're using pulp, it's quicker to buy a ready-made, dried mix, to which you simply add water. On the whole, paper strip papier mâché is the easiest to make and handle. The containers shown on these pages are all made in this way and decorated on a marine theme in a lively, contemporary style.

These papier mâché dishes, decorated with stylized fish motifs, show how you can develop a theme to create an outstanding design collection. The pedestal bowl is created by joining together large and small moulded shapes.

PAPER STRIP PAPIER MACHE

With the paper strip method of papier mâché, you simply coat torn strips of newspaper with a mixture of wallpaper paste and PVA adhesive and apply them in layers over your chosen mould, such as a mixing bowl from the kitchen. With each layer the torn paper strips fuse together and dry to form a strong, rigid shape. Once the shape is set, you ease the papier mâché form from its mould, and use more pasted strips to attach decorative details, such as pedestals and handles, to create design variations. Then you sand down the surfaces until they are smooth in preparation for decorating with paint or decoupage.

DECORATING PAPIER MACHE

The simplest way to decorate papier mâché is with water-based paints such as household emulsion (latex) and artists' acrylic paint. A base coat of pale coloured emulsion provides an opaque background ready for you to paint on your design.

To create an effect like the boldly defined fish motifs shown here, use a resist medium such as masking fluid (available from art shops) to draw the design. Paint over it with a rich colour wash to create the background then, when dry, peel away the masking fluid to reveal the motifs.

MAKING A PAPIER MACHE DISH

YOU WILL NEED

- ❖ LARGE MIXING BOWL as a mould
- ❖ SMALL BOWL (optional base)
- ❖ PETROLEUM JELLY (VASELINE)
- ❖ OLD NEWSPAPERS
- ❖ WALLPAPER ADHESIVE
- ❖ PVA ADHESIVE
- ❖ CONTAINER WITH LID
- ❖ SPOON
- ❖ SHARP SCISSORS
- ❖ WHITE/MINERAL SPIRIT
- ❖ WOOD ADHESIVE
- ❖ MEDIUM and FINE SANDPAPER
- ❖ WHITE EMULSION/LATEX PAINT
- ❖ SMALL HOUSEHOLD PAINT BRUSH
- ❖ WHITE MASKING FLUID
- ❖ ACRYLIC PAINT – small tube of turquoise and cobalt blue
- ❖ PLATE for mixing paint
- ❖ MEDIUM ACRYLIC BRISTLE BRUSH
- ❖ CLEAR, MATT FINISH ACRYLIC WOOD VARNISH

1 Preparing the moulds Apply a generous coating of petroleum jelly to the inside of the large bowl, taking it right over the lip. If you wish to make a pedestal for the dish, repeat the procedure with the small bowl or mould.

3 Adding the first layer Paste both sides of a paper strip and lay it across the centre of the large bowl, overhanging it on each side. Smooth it flat. Paste another strip and lay it at right angles to the first strip. Lay two more pasted strips diagonally across the bowl between the first two strips. Fill the gaps between these strips with shorter strips, overhanging the sides as before, but not covering the centre as this would make the base too thick.

2 Tearing the paper strips Tear the paper into 2.5-4cm (1-1½in) wide strips, long enough to overhang both sides of the large bowl by at least 5cm (2in) when laid in place inside. In the container, mix up the wallpaper paste to full strength, and stir in a little PVA adhesive until the mixture is a light, creamy colour. Place the lid on the container until you are ready to use the mixture.

4 Finishing the first layer Smooth extra paste over the strips with your fingers to fuse the paper together, pressing out any air bubbles. Press the paper to the edge of the bowl, making sure it does not adhere to the outside. Use scissors to trim the overhang to 2.5cm (1in).

5 Adding the second layer Before the first layer dries, tear several paper strips into rough squares. Moisten them on both sides with paste and stick them over the first layer, covering it completely. At the edges, rub the layers together between your fingers and thumb, then smooth extra paste over the surface as in step 4. Trim the overhang as necessary.

Once the papier mâché dish is sanded down and covered with two coats of white emulsion it has a fairly smooth surface for decorating. In this case, the fish design is drawn in masking fluid before the whole dish is colourwashed in turquoise and cobalt blue paints. When dry, the masking fluid is peeled away to reveal the white outlines of the fish swimming round the bowl.

6 Adding more layers Repeat steps 3-5 three more times, pressing out air bubbles and trimming the overhang between each layer, and then finish with a strip layer; you should have a total of nine paper layers on the bowl. Strengthen the top edge of the bowl with a layer of pasted squares, then pinch together to form a ridge, making sure that the paper does not stick to the outside of the bowl. If you are making a pedestal for the bowl, repeat steps 2-6 on the smaller bowl.

▼▲▼ T I P ▼▲▼

DECORATING WITH PAPER

Instead of using paints to decorate your papier mâché dishes, you can use coloured papers to create designs by just sticking them in place. Use a bold mix of vibrantly coloured foils or art papers to create a lively abstract design; or motifs cut from giftwrap and wallpaper – either closely overlapped or spaced out over a painted background – for an eye-catching decoupaged finish. Protect the dish with several coats of clear varnish.

7 Drying and unmoulding Leave the papier mâché to dry in a warm place such as an airing cupboard, but away from direct heat, for at least two days. Test to see if the paper is dry by gently inserting a blunt knife between the bowl and the papier mâché. If it releases easily it is ready, if not, leave for another 24 hours before unmoulding it. Let the unmoulded papier mâché dry out completely for a further day, then rub the surface with white spirit to remove any petroleum jelly residue.

8 Neatening the edges Using sharp scissors and following the lip at the top edge, cut away the excess. Reinforce the cut edge with small pieces of pasted newspaper, smoothing them down so that they stick. Leave to dry.

9 Adding a pedestal base (optional) Spread woodworking adhesive on the base of your small papier mâché bowl, and press it centrally on to the base of the larger bowl. Allow the adhesive to set. To neaten the join, make a roll from a couple of pasted paper strips, then paste them round the join. Stick the roll in place with small pasted pieces of paper. Smooth over with extra paste and leave it to dry.

10 Finishing off Gently smooth the surface of the dish with medium sandpaper, then finish with fine sandpaper. Paint the dish with two coats of white emulsion paint. The first coat of paint may crack, but the second coat covers smoothly. Leave the dish to dry completely.

PAINTING A FISH DESIGN

You need to work quickly with masking medium as it dries fast. Dampen the brush with water regularly to keep the medium flowing, and work long lines in a series of short strokes. Practise on scrap paper first.

1 Painting the fish Decide how to position the fish. Use masking medium and a watercolour brush to paint each fish body and tail in two strokes. Finish off the tail and paint the fins. Next paint the eye, gills and scales. Fill in between the fish with swirls and wavy lines, then paint a simple line round the top edge or the centre of the bowl. If you make a mistake, just peel away the dried fluid and start again.

2 Painting the colour wash Squeeze out some turquoise and cobalt blue acrylic paint on to an old plate. Working quickly, use a very damp brush to work one colour at random over the inside of the dish, leaving patches of white. Apply the other colour immediately, covering some of the first colour and the remaining white background. To darken the effect, repeat the process after the first coat is dry.

3 Painting the outside Once the inside of the dish is dry, turn it over and apply the colours to the outside in the same way. Leave it to dry then turn it right side up.

4 Finishing off Gently rub and peel off the masking fluid to reveal the white design underneath. Apply at least four coats of acrylic varnish inside and outside the dish, allowing each coat to dry thoroughly for about two hours before applying the next.

PAPIER MACHE VASE

Use an inexpensive glass or plastic container as a permanent mould inside a decorative papier mâché covering – then you can fill the vase with water for fresh flower displays.

1 Covering the container mould Follow *Making a Papier Mâché Dish*, step 2, to prepare the paper strips and paste. There is no need to grease the container mould before you start, as you won't be removing it at the end. Apply and finish the papier mâché as for *Making a Papier Mâché Dish*, steps 3-10, but work the strips over the outside of the container and down inside the neck for as far as they can be seen.

2 Working the design Use acrylic paints to paint the design. To copy the seashore inspired design shown here, paint the background in a warm, sandy colour, then use a pencil to mark on the design motifs lightly. Paint these with a watercolour brush in a mixture of darker, toning colours, then seal the finished design with varnish as in step 4, *Painting a Fish Design*.

A ribbed glass vase acquires a completely new image when covered with papier mâché and painted with a simple seashore design.

Papier Mache Accessories

Use a simple technique to sculpt a menagerie of papier mâché accessories – handles, hooks and light pulls – from pulp made from newspaper.

There are two techniques for making papier mâché, one using torn strips of paper which you paste together in layers, and the other using paper pulp. You can buy ready-made pulp mix, to which you just add water, but it's more fun and a lot less expensive to make your own.

To make papier mâché pulp you need to shred paper into small fragments, boil and mash it, and then blend it with adhesive. The resulting thick purée has a clay-like consistency which you can mould or sculpt with your hands or with tools to form various shapes. Once the pulp is dry it is lightweight but very firm and slightly more substantial than strip papier mâché.

As pulp allows you to build up shapes and sculpt fairly intricate details it's an ideal medium for these animal-shaped accessories. And, although it's not indestructible, it should be tough enough to withstand the rough and tumble of daily use in a child's room.

You can use almost any type of paper for the pulp, from egg boxes to newspaper – though some types are easier to mash up than others. Coarse-grained paper produces a textured pulp while fine paper, like tissue, produces pulp with a smooth finish. These accessories are all made with newspaper pulp which is cheap, fairly easy to mash up and has a gnarled texture. If you prefer a smoother finish you can sand the surface once it is dry.

Painted in bright colours to suit a playroom or child's bedroom, these figurative animal accessories – used as drawer handles and pegs – are akin to the cheery paper dolls of Indian and Mexican folk art.

PULP PAPIER MACHE

As well as paper and PVA adhesive, the recipe for pulp papier mâché needs a few extra ingredients. Linseed oil makes the pulp stronger and easier to work, plaster of Paris acts as a filler and whitener, wallpaper adhesive binds the pulp and prevents it from rotting, and oil of cloves also helps stop the pulp rotting.

Cardboard cutouts create a frame for all the papier mâché accessories featured here. The cardboard gives a firm flat surface to build the pulp on, an outline for the shape you are sculpting and, if necessary, a base to fix the knob on to. To strengthen the card and hide the holes in the edge of corrugated card, cover it with two or three layers of strip papier mâché before applying the pulp.

1 Soaking the paper Tear the newspaper into small pieces, no larger than 2.5cm (1in) square. Place the paper in a large saucepan with enough water to cover it and leave it to soak overnight. Add 2 litres (4 pints) of water to the saucepan and bring it to the boil; simmer for two hours and then allow it to cool.

2 Blending the paper Blend the paper to a purée using either a hand-held electric whisk directly in the saucepan, or by placing small batches of the mixture in a blender. To avoid straining the blender motor turn it on in short bursts, no more than 15 seconds long.

3 Straining the pulp Use a sieve to strain most of the water from the pulp. Take handfuls of pulp and squeeze out more water until it has a soft clay-like consistency. Do not squeeze out too much water or the pulp will become too hard and unworkable. Add a little more water to the pulp if it starts to feel too dry.

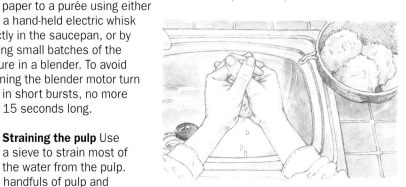

4 Mixing the pulp Place the pulp in a large mixing bowl or bucket. Add 2 tablespoons PVA adhesive, 1 tablespoon linseed oil, 1 tablespoon plaster of Paris and 2 drops oil of cloves, and mix thoroughly. Then sprinkle in 2 tablespoons of wallpaper adhesive and stir it in well.

T I P

STORING PULP
You can store any unused papier mâché pulp in an airtight container in the fridge. It remains workable for up to three weeks.

Newspaper papier mâché pulp makes a fun chunky texture for these animal drawer handles. If you prefer a smoother finish, sand the surface with fine-grade abrasive paper before painting the shapes.

PAPIER MACHE HANDLES

To make the drawer handles you need to glue a knob to the cardboard base and build strip and pulp papier mâché over the base and knob. Whether you're using your own design or the animal templates shown below, make sure you cut the base larger than the diameter of the knob. Use the knob as part of the shape you're creating – on the animals it becomes a rounded belly or face, or a dome-shaped back.

1 Cutting a cardboard base Draw your own template or if necessary use a photocopier to enlarge one of the templates below to the desired size. Trace the template on to cardboard and cut it out. Depending on the shape you are making, mark the position of the knob. Cut a hole at the mark, just large enough to fit the stem of the knob. Fit the stem into the hole and stick it in place with PVA.

2 Strengthening the base Mix up a small amount of wallpaper adhesive and stir in a little PVA. Tear narrow strips of newspaper and, following the method for strip papier mâché, use the paper and adhesive to cover the cardboard base and the stem of the knob. Make sure you cover the cardboard corrugations as well.

3 Sculpting the animals Taking small lumps at a time, build up the papier mâché pulp over the base and knob. Use your fingers to sculpt the pulp into shape. Leave the papier mâché to dry thoroughly for at least three days in a warm, ventilated place, such as an airing cupboard.

4 Painting a base coat Use a medium size paint brush to apply two coats of white emulsion to the papier mâché, allowing each coat to dry. Using a soft pencil and the template as a guide, mark the outlines and details of the animals or other design on to the papier mâché.

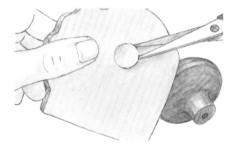

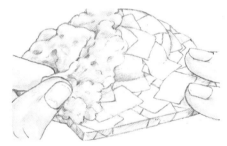

5 Colouring in the animals Using acrylic paints and an artists' fine brush, decorate the papier mâché. Paint the main colour areas first, then the smaller areas, and finally add the black details. Allow the paint to dry and apply two coats of clear acrylic varnish to seal. Allow to dry.

To make these papier mâché light pulls, sandwich a length of cord, knotted at the end, between two cut-out cardboard shapes. Then sculpt the shape with strip and pulp papier mâché and decorate with bright paint.

6 Fixing the handles Screw the knobs in place on the drawer or cupboard front. If there are no holes present, measure and mark the knob positions then use an electric drill and appropriate size wood twist bit to drill a hole through the wood at the marks.

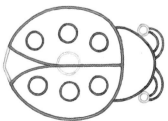

Papier Mache Hooks

To make these papier mâché hooks you need all of the materials previously listed for making handles, plus a short length of 2 x 1cm (¾ x ⅜in) wooden batten to strengthen the cardboard, two mirror plates and a tenon saw. For the hook itself use a metal coat hook or a wooden drawer knob – choose one that has a long stem. Position the strengthening batten vertically down the middle of the cardboard base and fix the knob to this so that it will bear the weight of any items hanging on the hook.

If you want to make stronger pegs – to carry a heavy overcoat, for instance – make the base from a piece of medium density fibreboard (MDF). Use a jigsaw to cut out the base, screw on a handle or hook and then decorate it with the pulp.

1 Making the base Draw your own design or use a photocopier to enlarge an animal template to the desired size. Trace the template on to corrugated cardboard and cut it out. Cut a second piece of card the same shape; stick the two pieces together with PVA adhesive. Mark the hook position on the cardboard base.

2 Cutting the batten Use the cardboard base itself to measure and mark off the length of batten you need. Position the batten vertically down the middle of the base, in line with the hook position. Use a pencil or felt-tip pen to mark off a length of batten about 1cm (⅜in) shorter than the base and then cut the batten at the mark with a tenon saw.

3 Fixing the hook Centre the batten vertically on the base and transfer the hook position on to the batten. Place the hook in position on the batten to mark the screw holes. Remove the batten and use a drill and wood twist bit to make the screw holes. Screw the hook to the batten. Use PVA adhesive to glue the batten in place on the front of the base.

4 Adding the papier mâché Following steps 1-4, *Pulp Papier Mâché*, make up the papier mâché pulp. Following steps 2-5, *Papier Mâché Handles*, cover the base, batten and stem of the hook with strip papier mâché and then sculpt the pulp papier mâché on top. Allow the pulp to dry for at least three days and nights, then paint and varnish the shapes.

5 Fixing the mirror plates Place mirror plates at either end of the batten on the back of the papier mâché, so the fixing holes just protrude from the edge. Mark the screw holes with a pencil or felt-tip pen, then remove the plates and use a bradawl to make pilot holes for the screws. Taking care not to damage the papier mâché, screw the mirror plates in place then screw to the wall.

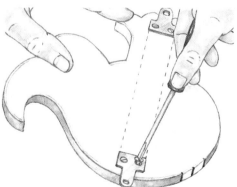

A spouting whale hook is a fun way of encouraging children into tidy habits.

COLOURING WICKERWORK

Compared to wooden furniture, wickerwork is relatively inexpensive.
Spray paint or a subtle wash of dye can brighten up a second-hand bargain,
and add an individual touch to a new piece.

Wickerwork is traditionally made from woven willow, but nowadays the term is used for items made from cane, rushes and rattan as well. It has always been popular as lightweight garden furniture and laundry baskets, but in recent years there has been a wickerwork boom, with exciting designs for just about every type of furniture and home accessory imaginable.

The popularity of wicker means that there is a wide choice of inexpensive wicker items available from chain stores. Or you may be able to pick up an interesting bargain from a car boot sale or second-hand store which you can stain or paint to make it look more distinctive.

Painting wicker is fairly straightforward. If the wicker is already painted or varnished, you must sand it down before you prime and paint it using either standard gloss or eggshell (flat satin) finish paint. Spray painting provides a better finish than paint applied with a brush because it gives a fine, even coverage without clogging up the weave.

If the paint finish on a piece of wicker is chipped with age, you don't have to re-paint all of it. You can simply sand and prime the damaged area, and touch it up with a small paint brush. If you have any trouble matching the colour, you can mix your own using small tubes of artists' oil paint.

Standard household dyes give wicker baskets a rich glow of colour – baskets dyed in this way make effective ornaments in their own right. Reduce or increase the strength of the dye to produce different depths of colour.

SPRAY-PAINTING WICKERWORK

Spray paint is the best choice if you want to colour large wicker items, such as furniture. The technique is quick and easy and, provided you take time to protect surrounding work surfaces, is far less messy than you'd think. It is also quite an economical way to revive an old piece, as one 400ml (14 fl oz) aerosol can is sufficient to cover a small chair.

◀ *A bright blue painted basket adds a lively touch to a pine dresser, on which a natural wicker basket would be lost.*

1 Cleaning the wicker If the wicker is dusty, clean it with your vacuum cleaner using a fine nozzle. Wearing rubber gloves to protect your hands, wash the wicker down with a weak solution of household bleach. Leave it to dry, preferably outside in the sun. Do not dry wicker over direct heat as this can cause it to crack.

2 Sanding down the surface Rub down the surface lightly with fine grade sandpaper. If the wicker is already painted, make sure that any flaky or chipped paint is sanded down to a smooth finish. Wipe it over with a soft duster.

3 Sealing the surface Protect all the surfaces with dust sheets. Apply one light coat of primer or undercoat, either with a brush or a spray. Leave it to dry thoroughly.

4 Painting the wicker Spray the wicker evenly with a thin layer of paint, following the manufacturer's instructions. Allow the paint to dry before applying a second and third coat.

USING SPRAY PAINT

If you haven't used spray paint before, bear in mind the following:
The paint fumes can be toxic, so work outdoors whenever possible. If you use spray paints indoors, make sure the room is well ventilated and wear a face mask for extra protection.

❖

The fine spray of paint from the aerosol canister tends to get everywhere. Spread plastic sheeting or dust sheets on the ground. Keep clear of brickwork and paths. Protect everything in the 'firing line', including the walls if you are painting indoors.

❖

Read the manufacturer's instructions on the paint can. Try out the spray on a piece of scrap paper first to ensure that the nozzle is clear.

❖

Hold the can the correct distance away from the wicker and spray across it in wide, horizontal sweeps. Keep the can moving to leave only a thin coating so the paint doesn't run or clog the weave.

❖

Three thin coats of paint look better than one thick one and are less likely to reveal chips. When the first coat of paint is dry, sand down any drips and lightly respray the area. Repeat once more.

❖

MULTICOLOURED PAINT EFFECTS

Once you have sprayed an overall background colour over your piece of wickerwork, you can add decorative detail in a contrasting colour with a brush.

Part of the charm of wickerwork is its bumpy, woven texture. Bands of colour that follow the direction of the weave and strong geometric patterns are more effective than delicate designs that tend to get broken up by the surface texture.

You can also create attractive effects by spraying paint through stencils, and by dabbing on paint with a sponge.

▼ *Brightly coloured wicker table and chairs add zest to a timber verandah and provide a welcoming setting for an informal meal. There's no rule that says all the pieces have to be the same colour – as this picture shows, a mismatched look is very effective.*

TIP

PAINTING LLOYD LOOM FURNITURE
Lloyd loom furniture looks like wickerwork but is actually made from paper twisted round a steel wire core. You should never sand it down or paint it with a brush because this ruins the surface. If you do need to touch up the painted finish, use spray paint. To find out whether a piece is a Lloyd loom, look for the trademark label underneath.

DYEING WICKERWORK

Untreated wicker absorbs coloured dyes well, unlike varnished pieces which do not take the dye. Any dark spots and colour variations in the wicker show through the dye and give the piece a charming, rustic look.

The most practical place to dye baskets and other small pieces is in a metal kitchen sink, or large metal pot, as here they can steep in the dye and acquire a strong colour. You can dye larger pieces too, but the process is time-consuming and messy if you do not have a large enough container to take the piece. Do not dye wicker in a good plastic container or an acrylic bath as the dye may permanently stain.

For the best results on small wicker pieces, use two containers of dye dissolved according to the manufacturer's instructions, although you may need a greater volume of dye for larger pieces. If you want a very pale colour, add more water to the solution. However, it is advisable to test the colour first. Remember that the wicker looks paler when it has dried.

YOU WILL NEED

❖ COLD WATER DYE and FIXATIVE

❖ LARGE MEASURING JUG

❖ METAL SPOON

❖ STIFF WASHING-UP BRUSH or SPONGE

❖ CLEAR SPRAY VARNISH

❖ WAX POLISH (optional)

❖ PLASTIC SHEETING

❖ RUBBER GLOVES

❖ PROTECTIVE CLOTHING

❖ BLEACH or CREAM CLEANER

1 Preparing the wicker Clean and lightly sand down the surface of old wicker to remove any grime and grease as in *Spray-painting Wickerwork,* steps 1 and 2. Wash new wicker in warm soapy water and leave it to dry thoroughly, preferably outside in the sun.

3 Dyeing the wicker Lay the wicker in the dye solution so the dye covers as much as possible. Using a clean brush or sponge, rub the colour over the wicker, turning it constantly so that it evenly absorbs as much dye as possible. When it is the required colour (this may take up to 20 minutes), transfer it to a protective plastic sheet to dry. Clean the sink with bleach or cream cleaner.

2 Mixing the dye Fit the plug in the sink. Use the jug to measure the quantity of water as given by the dye manufacturer. Wear rubber gloves and mix in the dye according to the manufacturer's instructions. To check the colour intensity, dab a little on the wicker in a place where it does not show. If it is too strong, add a little extra water.

4 Sealing the surface Spray your dyed wicker with gloss or satin varnish to enhance the colour and to prevent any colour rubbing off and staining other surfaces. Alternatively, rub wax polish into the weave and buff it to a shine.

DYEING LARGE OBJECTS

Spread a large piece of plastic sheeting over the ground and stand the piece of wicker in the middle. Using a sponge, carefully rub the diluted dye over the surface, turning the piece over as necessary. Mop up the dye from the plastic as you work and re-apply it. If necessary, use a brush to rub the dye into the weave. Continue applying and rubbing in the dye as necessary, then drain on clean plastic until dry.

◁ *Dyed baskets have many uses, from simple display pieces to decorative containers for all sorts of household objects. Here the muted tones of purple provide a perfect setting for the vivid tones of heather.*